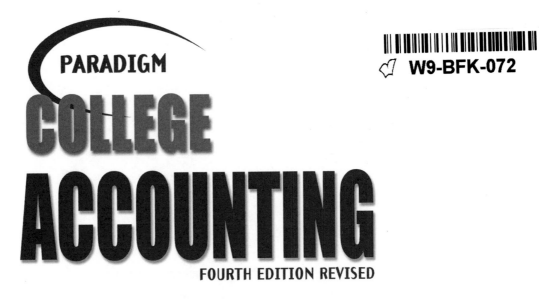

PARADIGM
COLLEGE
ACCOUNTING
FOURTH EDITION REVISED

W9-BFK-072

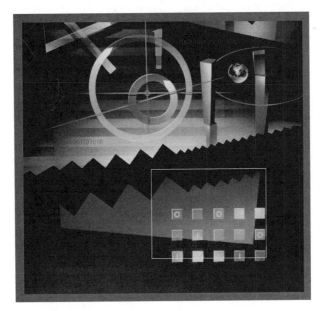

STUDY GUIDE AND WORKING PAPERS
Chapters 19–29

Robert L. Dansby, Ph.D.
Columbus Technical College • Columbus, Georgia

Burton S. Kaliski, Ed.D.
Southern New Hampshire University • Manchester, New Hampshire

Michael D. Lawrence, MBA, CPA, CMA
Portland Community College • Portland, Oregon

EMCParadigm
PUBLISHING

ACKNOWLEDGMENT

The authors and publisher wish to thank Sherry Cohen for her excellent work in editing the chapter summaries and practice tests.

Cover Image: Roy Weinman, Image Bank.

ISBN: 0-7638-2004-0
C/N: 28610

CONTENTS

Corporate Accounting—Formation and Paid-In Capital

CHAPTER SUMMARY

A **corporation** is a form of business that is owned by investors. The owners of a corporation are called **stockholders** (or **shareholders**), and their investments are referred to as the **capital stock** (or **stock**) of the corporation. The corporate form of business is well suited to raising large amounts of capital because corporations can sell stock to many thousands of investors, if it is **publicly held**. Thus, corporations, generally speaking, are larger—in terms of earnings, assets owned, and people employed—than sole proprietorships and partnerships. However, not all corporations are large; some have fewer than five stockholders and may be closely held by this small group.

Certain characteristics distinguish corporations from sole proprietorships and partnerships. Some of these characteristics serve as advantages; others act as disadvantages. The characteristics that are chiefly advantages are separate legal entity status, **limited liability** of owners (stockholders), ease of raising capital, ease of change of ownership, no mutual agency, and professional management. The characteristics that are chiefly disadvantages are double taxation and a greater amount of government regulation. Double taxation occurs because a corporation must pay an income tax on its net earnings. When a part of after-tax earnings is distributed to stockholders as **dividends**, the stockholders must report the dividends as personal income when filing state and federal income tax returns.

A corporation is created when a state grants a corporate **charter** to the organizers (incorporators) of the corporation who have filed the **articles of incorporation**. The organizers then agree on **bylaws**, call a meeting of stockholders, and elect a **board of directors** who appoint the corporate managers.

There are two basic forms of corporate capital: **paid-in capital** and **earned capital**. When these two types of capital are presented on the balance sheet, they are collectively referred to as **stockholders' equity**. Paid-in capital represents the amount of assets contributed to the corporation by the owners through the owners' purchase of the corporation's capital stock. Earned capital arises from profitable operations and is presented on the balance sheet as **retained earnings**. Earned capital represents earnings that have been reinvested in the corporation.

The corporate charter indicates the **authorized stock** of the corporation. Shares sold are **issued stock**. Shares that continue to be held by investors are **outstanding stock**.

There are two basic types of capital stock: **common stock** and **preferred stock**. If a corporation issues only one type of stock, it will be common stock. To appeal to a larger range of investors, however, many corporations issue stock that has certain preference features over common stock. Such stock is referred to as preferred stock and usually has preference over common stock in two ways: (1) preferred stockholders are entitled to share in corporate earnings first when the board of directors declares a dividend, and (2) preferred stockholders have a prior claim to the assets of a corporation if the corporation is forced to liquidate. Common stockholders, however, have a **pre-emptive right** to buy new shares of stock.

Preferred stock can be issued with a variety of characteristics. **Cumulative preferred stock** refers to preferred stock in which a stated dividend accumulates from year to year. Thus, if stated dividends are not paid in the current year, they become **dividends in arrears** and must be paid in subsequent years before common shareholders receive anything. **Noncumulative preferred stock** refers to preferred stock that does not accumulate dividends. Thus, in years in which the board of directors decides not to pay a dividend—which often happens when earnings are low or when the corporation is expanding and needs all available capital—the dividend is lost forever to the holders of noncumulative preferred stock and common stock. Most preferred stock is cumulative.

Participating preferred stock refers to preferred stock that has a right to a stated dividend and, after common stock has been paid a dividend, can participate in any excess dividends. **Nonparticipating preferred stock** does not have this right.

When a corporation is chartered, it specifies the type of stock it wishes to sell. Also a face value is often assigned to each share of stock. The face value, called **par value**, is simply a way of dividing ownership into individual shares. Any amount can be assigned as the par value, which appears on each **stock certificate**. The most significant aspect of par value is that it provides legal capital. **Legal capital**, which is usually equal to the par value of the shares outstanding, is an amount of paid-in capital that must be retained before a dividend can be paid to stockholders. This gives a minimum level of protection to creditors because the creditors of a corporation cannot look beyond the assets of the corporation in settling debts.

Stock can also be issued with no-par value, and **no-par value stock** can have a **stated value**. In accounting, there is little difference between par value stock and stated value stock.

Capital stock may be issued at par, above par, or below par. Par value is not an indicator of market value—it is strictly a legal matter. When stock is issued above or below par, the excess or deficiency is recorded in a **premium account** called **Paid-in Capital in Excess of Par**, or, if no balance exists in this account, in a **discount** account. Stock can be issued for cash, plant assets, legal services, or on account.

Capital stock that is reacquired by a corporation is termed **treasury stock**. Stock can be reacquired for various reasons, such as to have shares available for distribution to employees under stock option plans or bonus plans, and to support the market price of the stock by stimulating trading in it. If treasury stock is resold, no gain or loss is recognized on the exchange.

PRACTICE TEST

PART I TRUE/FALSE

Please circle the correct answer.

T   F   1. The corporate form of business permits the accumulation of large amounts of capital through the sale of stock to many thousands of investors.

T   F   2. A corporation is created by law as an entity separate and apart from its owners.

T   F   3. The owners of a corporation, like the partners in a partnership, have unlimited liability.

T   F   4. The life of a corporation is not related to the lives of its owners.

T   F   5. All owners of a corporation must approve any transfer of ownership between stockholders.

T   F   6. Stockholders, acting as owners, cannot enter into contracts that would be binding on the corporation.

T   F   7. The earnings of a corporation are taxed twice, once on the corporation's tax return and once on the stockholders' returns when they report dividends.

T   F   8. The organizers of a corporation must apply to the state for a charter in order to operate their business as a corporation.

T   F   9. Organization costs are debited to an expense account and charged against earnings in the first year of a corporation's existence.

T   F 10. The stockholders of a corporation must hire the management of the corporation.

T   F 11. The board of directors is elected by the stockholders.

T   F 12. In accounting for corporate capital, paid-in or invested capital is kept separate from earned capital.

T   F 13. A corporation may not issue any more shares of stock than is permitted by its charter.

T   F 14. The term *issued* is a financial term used to describe the sale of stock.

T   F 15. Preferred stock is the stock that gets to vote first.

T   F 16. Common stock is the residual ownership of the corporation.

T   F 17. Preferred stock has a claim to dividends before common stock.

T   F 18. Par value is an arbitrary amount assigned to each share of stock by the corporate charter.

T   F 19. Par value and market value are the same.

T   F 20. All states allow stock to be sold at less than its par value.

PART II MATCHING

Please match each of the following terms with its definition.

a. articles of incorporation
b. authorized stock
c. capital stock
d. charter
e. common stock
f. corporation
g. cumulative
h. dividends
i. dividends in arrears
j. issued stock

k. limited liability
l. outstanding stock
m. paid-in capital
n. par value
o. participating
p. preferred stock
q. retained earnings
r. stockholders
s. stockholders' equity
t. treasury stock

_____ 1. Those who possess stock in a corporation.

_____ 2. An application filed with the state to form a corporation.

_____ 3. The earnings of a corporation that are distributed to the stockholders.

_____ 4. The amount of accumulated earnings that a corporation has not paid out to stockholders.

_____ 5. Shares of ownership of a corporation.

_____ 6. Shares that have been sold to stockholders.

_____ 7. The number of shares actually in the hands of stockholders.

_____ 8. A class of stock that has special rights that common stock does not have, such as a prior claim to dividends.

_____ 9. Undeclared dividends on cumulative preferred stock that must be paid before common stock dividends.

_____ 10. A fixed amount for each share of stock that is stated in the corporate charter.

_____ 11. A form of business that has all the legal rights and responsibilities of an individual except the right to vote.

_____ 12. Stockholders are not liable for the debts incurred by the corporation.

_____ 13. A contract between the state and the incorporators creating the corporation.

_____ 14. Capital that comes from stockholders through the sale of stock.

_____ 15. The owners' claims against the assets of the corporation.

_____ 16. Shares of the corporation's own stock that are reacquired by the corporation.

_____ 17. The voting stock of the corporation; the stock with residual equity.

_____ 18. The type of preferred stock that allows unpaid dividends to accumulate from year to year.

_____ 19. The type of preferred stock that allows it to receive more than its fixed dividend under certain circumstances.

_____ 20. The maximum number of shares of stock that a corporation is permitted to sell according to its charter.

PART III FILL IN THE BLANKS

Please complete each sentence with the correct word or words.

1. The people elected by the stockholders to run the corporation make up the _____.

2. The capital that comes from profitable operations of the business is _____.

3. Preferred stock in which the dividend is limited to a fixed amount is called _____.

4. The amount of capital that a corporation must retain for the protection of its creditors is called _____.

5. A stock without a fixed dollar value assigned to each share is _____ stock.

6. A(n) _____ is similar to a par value.

7. When stock is sold at an amount above par value, the additional capital is credited to an account entitled _____.

8. When stock is sold for less than par, it is sold at a(n) _____.

9. Common stockholders have a(n) _____ claim to the assets of the corporation.

10. The right of common stockholders to maintain their proportionate ownership share of the corporation is called the _____ right.

PART IV MULTIPLE CHOICE

Please circle the correct answer.

1. When stock is sold on a subscription basis,
   a. the stock is issued right away.
   b. the stock is issued after full payment is received.
   c. the stock may be voted and receive dividends right away.
   d. none of the above.

2. Treasury stock is
   a. unissued stock.
   b. outstanding stock.
   c. issued stock that has been reacquired by the issuing corporation.
   d. none of the above.

3. The Treasury Stock account is
   a. a contra stockholders' equity account.
   b. an asset account.
   c. a liability account.
   d. a contra asset account.

4. Treasury stock
   a. may be voted by the corporation.
   b. may receive dividends when declared by the corporation.
   c. may not be voted or receive dividends.
   d. is the same as unissued stock.

5. The Organization Costs account is
   a. an asset account with a debit balance.
   b. an expense account with a debit balance.
   c. a liability account with a credit balance.
   d. a stockholders' equity account with a credit balance.

6. The Common Stock Subscribed account is
   a. an asset account with a debit balance.
   b. an expense account with a debit balance.
   c. a liability account with a credit balance.
   d. a stockholders' equity account with a credit balance.

7. The Paid-In Capital in Excess of Par account is
   a. an asset account with a debit balance.
   b. an expense account with a debit balance.
   c. a liability account with a credit balance.
   d. a stockholders' account with a credit balance.

8. Two advantages of a corporation are
   a. limited life and mutual agency.
   b. unlimited liability and division of responsibility.
   c. continuity of life and ease of raising capital.
   d. double taxation and more government regulation.

9. Two disadvantages of a corporation are
   a. limited life and mutual agency.
   b. unlimited liability and division of responsibility.
   c. continuity of life and ease of raising capital.
   d. double taxation and more government regulation.

10. On a corporation's balance sheet, there is
    a. a capital account for each stockholder.
    b. a capital account for each class of stock, for amounts invested over par value, and for the retained earnings of the corporation.
    c. a capital account for organization costs.
    d. a capital account for amounts due on subscribed stock.

PART V WRITING/SHORT ANSWER

1. **Reflect** Make a list, in words or simple phrases, of the most important and meaningful points in this chapter.

2. **Question** Think about the most confusing points or the material you do not understand in this chapter. Write down two or three questions that remain unanswered.

3. **Connect** Explain, in one or two sentences, the connection between the main points of this chapter and the major goals of the entire course.

4. **Summarize** Review this chapter's Joining the Pieces visual summary and explain the concept(s) illustrated in a few sentences.

WORKING PAPERS

SKILLS REVIEW

EXERCISE 19-1

General Journal Page 1

	Date	Account Title	P.R.	Debit	Credit	
1						1
2						2
3						3
4						4
5						5

EXERCISE 19-2

1. **General Journal** Page 1

	Date	Account Title	P.R.	Debit	Credit	
1						1
2						2
3						3
4						4
5						5
6						6
7						7
8						8
9						9
10						10
11						11

2. _____

EXERCISE 19-3

General Journal Page 1

	Date	Account Title	P.R.	Debit	Credit	
1						1
2						2
3						3
4						4

EXERCISE 19-4

General Journal

Page 1

	Date		Account Title	P.R.	Debit	Credit	
1							1
2							2
3							3
4							4
5							5
6							6
7							7
8							8
9							9
10							10
11							11
12							12
13							13
14							14
15							15

EXERCISE 19-5

General Journal

Page 1

	Date		Account Title	P.R.	Debit	Credit	
1							1
2							2
3							3
4							4
5							5
6							6

EXERCISE 19-6

General Journal

Page 1

	Date		Account Title	P.R.	Debit	Credit	
1							1
2							2
3							3
4							4
5							5

EXERCISE 19-7

General Journal

Page 1

	Date		Account Title	P.R.	Debit	Credit	
1							1
2							2
3							3
4							4
5							5
6							6
7							7
8							8
9							9
10							10
11							11
12							12
13							13
14							14

EXERCISE 19-8

General Journal

Page 1

	Date		Account Title	P.R.	Debit	Credit	
1							1
2							2
3							3
4							4
5							5
6							6
7							7
8							8
9							9
10							10
11							11
12							12
13							13

EXERCISE 19-9

PROBLEM 19-2A OR 19-2B

	Date		Account Title	P.R.	Debit	Credit	
1							1
2							2
3							3
4							4
5							5
6							6
7							7
8							8
9							9
10							10
11							11
12							12
13							13
14							14
15							15
16							16
17							17
18							18
19							19
20							20
21							21
22							22
23							23
24							24
25							25
26							26
27							27
28							28
29							29
30							30
31							31
32							32

General Journal

	Date		Account Title	P.R.	Debit	Credit	
1							1
2							2
3							3
4							4
5							5
6							6
7							7
8							8
9							9
10							10
11							11
12							12
13							13
14							14
15							15
16							16
17							17
18							18
19							19
20							20
21							21
22							22
23							23
24							24
25							25
26							26
27							27
28							28
29							29
30							30
31							31
32							32
33							33
34							34

PROBLEM 19-4A OR 19-4B

1. Amount of retained earnings: _____

2. Number of preferred shares issued: _____
   Number of common shares issued: _____

3. Number of subscribed common shares: _____

4.

This page intentionally left blank.

CHALLENGE PROBLEMS

PROBLEM SOLVING

1. Legal capital requirement = _____

2.

This page intentionally left blank.

COMMUNICATIONS

_____

_____

_____

_____

_____

_____

_____

_____

_____

_____

_____

_____

_____

_____

_____

_____

_____

ETHICS

_____

_____

_____

_____

_____

_____

_____

_____

_____

_____

_____

_____

_____

_____

_____

_____

_____

_____

This page intentionally left blank.

PRACTICE TEST ANSWERS

PART I

1. T
2. T
3. F
4. T
5. F
6. T
7. T
8. T
9. T
10. F
11. T
12. T
13. T
14. T
15. F
16. T
17. T
18. T
19. F
20. F

PART II

1. r
2. a
3. h
4. q
5. c
6. j
7. l
8. p
9. i
10. n
11. f
12. k
13. d
14. m
15. s
16. t
17. e
18. g
19. o
20. b

PART III

1. board of directors
2. earned capital
3. nonparticipating
4. legal capital
5. no-par value
6. stated value
7. Paid-In Capital in Excess of Par
8. discount
9. residual
10. preemptive

PART IV

1. b
2. c
3. a
4. c
5. b
6. d
7. d
8. c
9. d
10. b

PART V

Answers will vary. Please discuss questions with your instructor.

20 Corporate Accounting—Earnings and Distribution

CHAPTER SUMMARY

This chapter introduces the concept of earned capital and the Retained Earnings account. Net income for a corporation flows through the closing process to Retained Earnings, which then may be distributed to the stockholders as dividends.

The closing process for corporations is very similar to the closing process for sole proprietorships and partnerships. Revenue and expense accounts are closed to the Income Summary account. The balance of the Income Summary account (the net income or net loss) is then closed to the Retained Earnings account. The balance of the Retained Earnings account represents the cumulative net income for a corporation, less losses and dividends.

The Retained Earnings account is a stockholders' equity account with a normal credit balance. As a result of net losses, however, a debit balance in Retained Earnings may occur. Such a balance is called a **deficit**.

Corporations are artificial persons. Consequently, a corporation must pay an income tax on its net earnings, just as real people do. This income tax is estimated at the beginning of the corporation's fiscal year and is paid throughout the year in quarterly installments. At year-end, the corporation's actual income tax for the year is calculated. The actual amount of income tax is then compared with the estimated tax. If any additional tax is owed, it must be paid within two and one-half months after the end of the corporation's fiscal year.

Dividends are distributions of corporate earnings to the stockholders of the company. There are three important dates associated with dividends: the **date of declaration**, the **date of record**, and the **date of payment**. The date of declaration is the date on which the dividend is actually declared by formal action of the board of directors. The date of record is the date set for determining the identity of the stockholders who will receive the dividend. The date of payment is the date on which the dividend is to be paid.

Preferred stockholders will receive their dividends before the common stockholders. Additionally, holders of cumulative preferred stock are entitled to receive any dividends in arrears, as well as current dividends, before common stockholders receive anything.

Most dividends are **cash dividends**. Corporations that wish to conserve cash and yet still pay a dividend will often declare a **stock dividend**. A stock dividend is a distribution of a corporation's own stock to stockholders of record. Stock dividends are usually distributions of common stock to common stockholders. It is possible to issue common stock to preferred stockholders or vice versa, but this is rare.

Stock splits occur when management wishes to reduce the market price of stock so that more investors can afford it. When stock is split, the par or stated value of the stock is reduced as well as the market value. However, the amounts in the paid-in capital accounts are not affected. Consequently, no journal entry—other than a **memorandum entry**—is needed to record the split.

The amount of a corporation's retained earnings that is available for dividends may be limited (or restricted) by the board of directors. The amount restricted is called an **appropriation of retained earnings**, and is recorded by transferring the amount from the Retained Earnings account to a Retained Earnings Appropriated account. An example of such an appropriation is Retained Earnings Appropriated for Plant Expansion. When the appropriation is no longer needed, it is returned to the Retained Earnings account.

At the end of an accounting period, corporations prepare a **retained earnings statement** to show how retained earnings changed during the period in question. The retained earnings statement usually shows the following:

Beginning retained earnings
Net income for the year
Dividends declared during the year
Changes in appropriations
Ending retained earnings

PRACTICE TEST

PART I TRUE/FALSE

Please circle the correct answer.

T F   1. Basic accounting for corporations differs from basic accounting for sole proprietorships and partnerships.

T F   2. In a corporation, when Income Summary is closed, the amount of the net income or net loss is transferred to Retained Earnings.

T F   3. When a corporation has a credit balance in Retained Earnings, that amount is legally available for dividends.

T F   4. A distribution of earnings to stockholders is called a withdrawal.

T F   5. The board of directors of a corporation is legally required to declare dividends every year.

T F   6. When a corporation declares a dividend, it becomes a liability to the corporation.

T F   7. One reason for a corporation to declare a stock dividend is to keep its cash on hand for use in expanding the business.

T F   8. When a dividend is declared, no journal entry is needed unless it is paid the same day.

T F   9. A journal entry is needed on the date of record to record the dividend.

T F   10. Payment of a dividend is handled just like payment of any other liability.

T F   11. When a corporation has preferred and common stock outstanding and a dividend is declared, the preferred stockholders must be paid first.

T F   12. Dividends in arrears are dividends owed to preferred stockholders because of the participating feature of preferred stock.

T F   13. If there are dividends in arrears on cumulative preferred stock, those dividends plus any current preferred dividends must be paid before dividends are paid on common stock.

T F   14. Holders of participating preferred stock have the right to participate in decisions made by the board of directors.

T F   15. A stock dividend is computed by multiplying the declared percentage dividend by the number of shares outstanding.

T F   16. The Stock Dividends account is debited for the par value of the additional shares to be distributed to stockholders.

T F   17. A stock split is usually declared to reduce the market price of the corporation's stock.

T F   18. A stock split removes retained earnings and transfers the amount to paid-in capital so that it is no longer available for dividends.

T F   19. When a corporation wants to show its shareholders that a certain amount of its assets is unavailable for dividends, the board of directors can appropriate the amount from retained earnings.

T F   20. A retained earnings statement is similar to a statement of owner's equity.

PART II MATCHING

Please match each of the following terms with its definition.

a. appropriation of retained earnings
b. cash dividend
c. date of declaration
d. date of payment
e. date of record

f. memorandum entry
g. Retained Earnings
h. deficit
i. stock dividend
j. stock split

_____ 1. A dividend paid in cash.

_____ 2. The date that the board of directors declares a dividend.

_____ 3. A change in a corporation's stock that occurs when the corporation recalls all of its stock and issues two, three, or more new shares in place of each old one.

_____ 4. The account that contains all the net income minus net losses and dividends that have accumulated in the corporation's history.

_____ 5. A journal entry in which an explanation of an event is recorded without any debits or credits to specific accounts.

_____ 6. The date that a dividend is paid.

_____ 7. The notice to stockholders and others that a certain amount of retained earnings is unavailable for dividends.

_____ 8. A dividend paid in shares of the corporation's own stock.

_____ 9. The date associated with reviewing the stockholders' records to determine the identity of the stockholders who are entitled to receive a dividend, how many shares they own, and their addresses.

_____ 10. A debit balance in the Retained Earnings account.

PART III FILL IN THE BLANKS

Please complete each sentence with the correct word or words.

1. The Income Summary account for a corporation is closed to the _____ account.

2. A distribution of earnings of a corporation to its shareholders is called a(n) _____.

3. A corporation does not have to pay dividends until the board of directors _____ them.

4. When a cash dividend is declared, a journal entry is made to debit _____ and credit _____.

5. Paying a dividend is just like paying any other _____.

6. A(n) _____ dividend is paid with shares of the corporation's own stock.

7. A stock dividend is strictly a stockholders' _____ transaction; there is no _____ involved in the payment.

8. Dividends are important to a corporation because they are one way to attract _____.

9. Holders of _____ preferred stock are entitled to receive dividends in arrears from past years before common stockholders can receive dividends.

10. Unless preferred stock is _____, it will not get more than its stated dividend.

11. A stock split has the effect of _____ the number of shares outstanding while _____ the par value of the shares.

12. A stock dividend moves _____ into _____ so that earnings are no longer available for cash dividends.

13. Neither a stock dividend nor a stock split will have any effect on _____ stockholders' equity.

14. A stock split requires only a(n) _____ entry in the journal.

15. When a corporation decides to use internal funds to finance growth, it often notifies its shareholders of this action by a(n) _____ of retained earnings.

16. When the need for a(n) _____ has passed, the entry is _____ and the amount is returned to the Retained Earnings account.

17. Some states require an appropriation of retained earnings to cover the cost of _____ stock.

18. A(n) _____ statement is similar to a statement of owner's equity.

19. The purpose of a(n) _____ statement is to explain the changes in retained earnings for the period.

20. The net income or net loss for the period, _____ paid, and _____ of retained earnings are shown on the retained earnings statement.

PART IV MULTIPLE CHOICE

Please circle the correct answer.

1. The Income Summary account of a corporation is closed to
   a. the individual capital accounts of all the stockholders.
   b. the Capital Stock account.
   c. the Retained Earnings account.
   d. none of the above.

2. The board of directors must consider many factors when declaring a dividend. Among them are:
   a. whether the corporation has enough retained earnings.
   b. whether the corporation is maintaining its dividend policy.
   c. whether there is enough cash to pay the dividend.
   d. all of the above.

3. There are three important dates associated with dividends. The two that require journal entries are
   a. the date of declaration and the date of payment.
   b. the date of declaration and the date of record.
   c. the date of record and the date of payment.
   d. the only journal entry required is on the date of payment.

4. A corporation has two ways of rewarding its shareholders with dividends. One way is strictly an equity transaction. It is
   a. a cash dividend.
   b. a stock split.
   c. a stock dividend.
   d. none of the above.

5. A stock split is different from a stock dividend in that
   a. a stock split moves retained earnings to paid-in capital.
   b. a stock split does not change the balance of any stockholders' equity account.
   c. a stock split requires a cash payment.
   d. a stock split is used only when the corporation does not have enough cash for a dividend.

6. Preferred stock that is entitled to its dividend from a prior year is
   a. cumulative.
   b. cumulative and participating.
   c. participating.
   d. noncumulative.

7. Preferred stock that is entitled to share in excess dividends with the common stock is
   a. cumulative.
   b. cumulative and participating.
   c. participating.
   d. noncumulative.

8. A notice to shareholders that a certain amount of retained earnings is not available for dividends is
   a. a memorandum entry.
   b. an appropriation.
   c. a notice of dividends in arrears.
   d. none of the above.

9. The retained earnings statement
   a. is similar to the statement of owner's equity.
   b. explains the changes in retained earnings for the period.
   c. shows the net income or net loss for the period, dividends, and appropriations.
   d. all of the above.

10. A corporation differs from a partnership or a sole proprietorship in that
    a. the owners of a corporation have unlimited liability.
    b. the corporation records invested capital and retained earnings in the same capital account.
    c. the corporation records invested capital and retained earnings in different capital accounts.
    d. the corporation allows owners to have a share of earnings.

PART V WRITING/SHORT ANSWER

1. **Reflect** Make a list, in words or simple phrases, of the most important and meaningful points in this chapter.

2. **Question** Think about the most confusing points or the material you do not understand in this chapter. Write down two or three questions that remain unanswered.

3. **Connect** Explain, in one or two sentences, the connection between the main points of this chapter and the major goals of the entire course.

4. **Summarize** Review this chapter's Joining the Pieces visual summary and explain the concept(s) illustrated in a few sentences.

WORKING PAPERS

SKILLS REVIEW

EXERCISE 20-1

General Journal   Page 1

	Date	Account Title	P.R.	Debit	Credit	
1						1
2						2
3						3
4						4
5						5
6						6
7						7
8						8
9						9
10						10

EXERCISE 20-2

_____

_____

_____

_____

_____

General Journal   Page 1

	Date	Account Title	P.R.	Debit	Credit	
1						1
2						2
3						3
4						4
5						5
6						6
7						7
8						8
9						9
10						10
11						11
12						12

EXERCISE 20-3

General Journal
Page 1

	Date		Account Title	P.R.	Debit	Credit	
1							1
2							2
3							3
4							4
5							5
6							6
7							7
8							8
9							9

EXERCISE 20-4

General Journal
Page 1

	Date	Account Title	P.R.	Debit	Credit	
1						1
2						2
3						3
4						4
5						5
6						6
7						7
8						8
9						9

EXERCISE 20-5

2.   **General Journal**   Page 1

	Date	Account Title	P.R.	Debit	Credit	
1						1
2						2
3						3
4						4
5						5

2.   **General Journal**   Page 1

	Date	Account Title	P.R.	Debit	Credit	
1						1
2						2
3						3
4						4
5						5

EXERCISE 20-6

General Journal   Page 1

	Date	Account Title	P.R.	Debit	Credit	
1						1
2						2
3						3
4						4
5						5
6						6
7						7
8						8
9						9
10						10

EXERCISE 20-7

General Journal

	Date		Account Title	P.R.	Debit	Credit	
1							1
2							2
3							3
4							4
5							5
6							6
7							7
8							8
9							9
10							10
11							11
12							12
13							13
14							14
15							15
16							16
17							17
18							18
19							19
20							20
21							21
22							22

EXERCISE 20-8

1. _____

2.

	Date	Account Title	P.R.	Debit	Credit	
1						1
2						2
3						3
4						4
5						5
6						6
7						7
8						8

General Journal — Page 1

3. _____

4. _____

5. _____

EXERCISE 20-9

General Journal — Page 1

	Date	Account Title	P.R.	Debit	Credit	
1						1
2						2
3						3
4						4
5						5
6						6
7						7
8						8
9						9
10						10
11						11
12						12
13						13

Allied Beverage Company										
Retained Earnings Statement										
For Year Ended December 31, 20X1										

CASE PROBLEMS

PROBLEM 20-1A OR 20-1B

1.

General Journal

Page 1

	Date	Account Title	P.R.	Debit	Credit	
1						1
2						2
3						3
4						4
5						5
6						6
7						7
8						8
9						9
10						10
11						11
12						12
13						13
14						14
15						15
16						16
17						17

2.

This page intentionally left blank.

CHALLENGE PROBLEMS

PROBLEM SOLVING

1. **General Journal** Page 1

	Date		Account Title	P.R.	Debit	Credit	
1							1
2							2
3							3
4							4
5							5
6							6
7							7
8							8
9							9
10							10
11							11
12							12
13							13
14							14
15							15
16							16
17							17
18							18
19							19
20							20
21							21
22							22
23							23
24							24
25							25
26							26
27							27
28							28
29							29
30							30
31							31
32							32

2.

Anderson Company Retained Earnings Statement For Year Ended December 31, 20X2														
	Unappropriated Retained Earnings					Appropriated for Contingencies								

3.

Anderson Company Balance Sheet December 31, 20X2												

COMMUNICATIONS

_____
_____
_____
_____
_____
_____
_____
_____
_____
_____
_____
_____
_____
_____
_____
_____
_____

ETHICS

_____
_____
_____
_____
_____
_____
_____
_____
_____
_____
_____
_____
_____
_____
_____
_____
_____
_____
_____

COMMUNICATIONS

This page intentionally left blank.

PRACTICE TEST ANSWERS

PART I

1. F
2. T
3. T
4. F
5. F
6. T
7. T
8. F
9. F
10. T
11. T
12. F
13. T
14. F
15. T
16. F
17. T
18. F
19. T
20. T

PART II

1. b
2. c
3. j
4. g
5. f
6. d
7. a
8. i
9. e
10. h

PART III

1. Retained Earnings
2. dividend

3. declares
4. Cash Dividends, Dividends Payable
5. liability
6. stock
7. equity, cash
8. investors
9. cumulative
10. participating
11. increasing, decreasing
12. retained earnings, paid-in capital
13. total
14. memorandum
15. appropriation
16. appropriation, reversed
17. treasury
18. retained earnings
19. retained earnings
20. dividends, appropriations

PART IV

1. c
2. d
3. a
4. c
5. b
6. a
7. c
8. b
9. d
10. c

PART V

Answers will vary. Please discuss questions with your instructor.

Long-Term Liabilities and Investments

CHAPTER SUMMARY

Corporations finance their operations by selling stock and by retaining earnings. Many corporations also finance or **leverage** their operations by issuing long-term debt. Long-term debt can generally be classified as *mortgage notes payable* and *bonds payable*. A mortgage note payable results when a corporation pledges a specific asset as security for a debt. A **bond** payable is, in reality, a long-term credit instrument that obligates the issuing corporation to repay the principal (**face value**) of the bond at **maturity**, as well as make periodic interest payments over the life of the bond. A **bond indenture** is the contract between the corporation and its **bond holders**.

Bonds can be classified in a variety of ways. For example, bonds can be classified as to the time of payment (**term bonds** or **serial bonds**), as to the type of security (**secured bonds** and **debenture bonds**), and as to the type of ownership (**registered bonds** and **coupon bonds**). Most bonds have characteristics of all these classifications.

Bonds are quoted on the bond market as a percent of face value. A bond quoted at 100 sells at face value; a bond quoted at 97 sells for 97% of face value. And a bond quoted at 102 sells for 102% of face value.

The typical face value of a bond in a **bond issue** is $1,000. However, a bond may or may not sell for face value. A bond can be sold for more than face value (at a **premium**), or a bond can be sold for less than face value (at a **discount**). There are several factors—such as the credit standing of the issuing corporation—that determine whether or not bonds sell for face value, above face value, or below face value. The overriding factor, however, is the interest rate the bond pays compared with the rate prevailing in the bond market. A bond sells for a premium when its contract rate is higher than the market rate. On the other hand, a bond sells at a discount when its **contract rate** is lower than the **market rate**.

If bonds are issued at face value, a journal entry is made to debit the Cash account and credit the Bonds Payable account. If bonds are issued for a premium, the amount of the premium is credited to the Premium on Bonds Payable account. If bonds are issued at a discount, the amount of the discount is debited to the Discount on Bonds Payable account. A premium or discount is amortized over the life of the bonds.

Bonds are reported in the Long-Term Liabilities section of the balance sheet. The balance of the Premium on Bonds Payable account is added to the related Bonds Payable account to obtain the carrying value of the bonds. Conversely, the balance of the Discount on Bonds Payable account is deducted from the related Bonds Payable account to obtain the carrying value of the bonds.

When corporations issue bonds between interest dates, the investor must pay the issuing corporation any interest accrued from the date of the bonds (or the date interest was last paid) to the date of purchase. In turn, the first interest payment to the bondholders will be for the full period. This practice simplifies the corporation's bookkeeping and avoids the expense of computing and paying interest for partial periods.

Corporations sometimes set up **sinking funds** to be better able to repay the principal of a bond issue at maturity. When sinking funds are used, cash is transferred annually from the general Cash account to the Sinking Fund Cash account. The sinking fund cash is then invested. Earnings from the sinking fund investments, along with the annual cash transfer, are reinvested in order to provide a cash fund that will be available to pay the bond issue at maturity.

Corporations often invest in other corporations. Investments in stocks are called **equity securities**; investments in bonds are called **debt securities**. Investments are recorded at their total cost, which includes any broker's fees necessary to acquire the investments. Earnings from investments are recorded in revenue accounts, as are gains when investments are sold for more than their carrying value.

How investments are presented on the balance sheet depends on whether management considers them to be **temporary investments** or **long-term investments**. Investments are considered temporary if (1) they can be easily converted to cash and (2) management intends to convert them to cash within one year. Temporary investments are listed on the balance sheet as current assets. Long-term investments are investments that management intends to hold longer than one year. Long-term investments are not intended as a ready source of cash and are listed on the balance sheet in the Investments section.

PRACTICE TEST

PART I TRUE/FALSE

Please circle the correct answer.

T F 1. Corporations are financed by selling corporate stock and by borrowing.

T F 2. Bonds are a form of short-term liability.

T F 3. Bonds require two types of payments: principal and interest.

T F 4. The maturity date of a bond is the date that the interest is due.

T F 5. Bond prices are quoted as a percent of face value.

T F 6. Bondholders are creditors of the corporation that issued the bonds.

T F 7. A coupon bond is registered by the issuing corporation so that the bondholder is protected from loss or theft.

T F 8. When a bond sells at more than face value, it is selling at a premium.

T F 9. A premium results when a bond is paying less interest than the market rate.

T F 10. When bonds are issued at other than face value, the Cash account is debited for the cash received, the Bonds Payable account is credited for the face amount, and a Premium or Discount on Bonds Payable account is credited or debited for the difference.

T F 11. Bonds always sell at the market price plus interest accrued since the last interest date.

T F 12. Any premium received from the sale of bonds is recorded as profit.

T F 13. Interest-bearing debts, such as bonds, require an adjusting entry for accrued interest at the end of an accounting period.

T F 14. Any premium or discount on bonds must be completely written off to revenue or expense at the end of the first period the bonds are outstanding.

T F 15. A bond sinking fund is similar to a savings account.

T F 16. Bond sinking fund accounts are assets to the corporation.

T F 17. Bonds are called equity securities.

T F 18. The commission paid a broker when purchasing stocks or bonds is added to the cost of the investment.

T F 19. Temporary investments should be reported on the balance sheet in the Current Assets section.

T F 20. When recording the purchase of stock for investment, it is necessary to separate par value from premium in the Investment account.

PART II MATCHING

Please match each of the following terms with its definition.

a. amortization
b. bond sinking fund
c. bond
d. coupon bonds
e. debenture bonds
f. debt securities
g. discount
h. equity securities
i. face interest rate
j. face value

k. long-term liabilities
l. market interest rate
m. marketable securities
n. maturity date
o. premium
p. registered bonds
q. retirement of bonds
r. secured bonds
s. serial bonds
t. term bonds

_____ 1. A form of long-term debt that requires two types of payments: principal and interest.

_____ 2. The date that a bond is repaid.

_____ 3. The amount of principal that must be repaid when a bond matures.

_____ 4. Bonds that mature all at one time.

_____ 5. Bonds that mature periodically over a number of years.

_____ 6. Bonds that have specific assets pledged as collateral.

_____ 7. Unsecured bonds that are based on the general credit rating of the corporation.

_____ 8. Bonds for which ownership is recorded with the issuing corporation so that the owners are protected against loss and theft.

_____ 9. Bearer bonds that are not registered with the issuing corporation.

_____ 10. The extra cash received by a corporation when its bonds are issued at more than face value.

_____ 11. The difference between face value and cash received when bonds are issued at less than face value.

_____ 12. The stated interest rate on bonds.

_____ 13. The prevailing interest rate for most bonds currently being sold on the bond market.

_____ 14. The systematic writing-off of the discount or premium on bonds to interest expense over the life of the bonds.

_____ 15. A fund, similar to a savings account, that is set up to pay off a bond issue at maturity.

_____ 16. Investments made by a corporation in the stock of other corporations.

_____ 17. Investments made by a corporation in the bonds of other corporations.

_____ 18. Securities that have a ready market and can be converted into cash quickly.

_____ 19. Debts that will not be repaid within one year or one accounting cycle.

_____ 20. The repayment of bonds.

PART III FILL IN THE BLANKS

Please complete each sentence with the correct word or words.

1. A $1,000 bond issued at 95½ would sell for $_____.

2. A $1,000 bond issued at 102¼ would sell for $_____.

3. The bond in Question 1 would be recorded by the issuing corporation as a debit to _____, a debit to _____, and a credit to _____.

4. Interest owed on bonds at the end of an accounting period must be _____ and an adjusting entry recorded.

5. Any premium or discount on bonds must be _____ over the life of the bonds.

6. A bond discount _____ the amount of interest expense for the corporation.

7. A bond sinking fund is reported as a(n) _____ on the balance sheet.

8. Temporary investments should be listed on the balance sheet as _____.

9. When an investment in stock is sold at more than its cost, a(n) _____ is reported on the income statement as _____ revenue.

10. When a dividend or interest is earned on an investment, it is reported as _____ on the income statement.

PART IV MULTIPLE CHOICE

Please circle the correct answer.

1. Bonds that are backed by only the good credit of the corporation are
   a. secured bonds.
   b. term bonds.
   c. debenture bonds.
   d. registered bonds.

2. When bonds are issued at a premium,
   a. Cash is debited, Premium on Bonds Payable is debited, and Bonds Payable is credited.
   b. Cash is debited, Premium on Bonds Payable is credited, and Bonds Payable is credited.
   c. Cash is credited and Investment in Bonds is debited.
   d. none of the above.

3. When bonds are issued between interest dates,
   a. the buyer pays accrued interest to the date of purchase.
   b. the seller pays accrued interest to the date of purchase.
   c. there is no interest recorded because none is due for payment.
   d. the issuing corporation will divide up the interest payment when it comes due.

4. When interest is paid on bonds that were issued at a discount,
   a. Cash is debited, Discount on Bonds Payable is debited, and Interest Expense is credited.
   b. Interest Expense is debited, Discount on Bonds Payable is credited, and Cash is credited.
   c. Cash is debited and Interest Income is credited.
   d. Interest Income is debited and Cash is credited.

5. At the end of the accounting period,
   a. interest expense must be accrued on outstanding bonds.
   b. interest income must be accrued on bond investments.
   c. the portion of the bond premium or discount related to the accrued interest expense must be amortized.
   d. all of the above.

6. To record a deposit in the bond sinking fund,
   a. Cash is debited and Bond Sinking Fund Cash is credited.
   b. Bond Sinking Fund Cash is debited and Cash is credited.
   c. Bond Investments is debited and Cash is credited.
   d. Bond Sinking Fund Revenue is debited and Cash is credited.

7. The entry to retire bonds when the sinking fund cash is less than the amount needed to pay the debt requires
   a. a debit to Bonds Payable, a credit to Bond Sinking Fund Cash, and a credit to Cash.
   b. a debit to Cash, a debit to Bond Sinking Fund Cash, and a credit to Bonds Payable.
   c. a debit to Bonds Payable and a credit to Cash.
   d. none of the above.

8. The bond discount or bond premium accounts are reported on the balance sheet in the
   a. Current Assets section.
   b. Long-Term Liabilities section.
   c. Investments section.
   d. Current Liabilities section.

9. Investments are classified as current or long-term based on
   a. the type of security held.
   b. the amount of income the security receives.
   c. how often the dividend or interest is received.
   d. the intent of management.

10. Marketable securities are listed on the balance sheet as
    a. long-term investments.
    b. sinking fund investments.
    c. current assets.
    d. current liabilities.

PART V WRITING/SHORT ANSWER

1. **Reflect** Make a list, in words or simple phrases, of the most important and meaningful points in this chapter.

2. **Question** Think about the most confusing points or the material you do not understand in this chapter. Write down two or three questions that remain unanswered.

3. **Connect** Explain, in one or two sentences, the connection between the main points of this chapter and the major goals of the entire course.

4. **Summarize** Review this chapter's Joining the Pieces visual summary and explain the concept(s) illustrated in a few sentences.

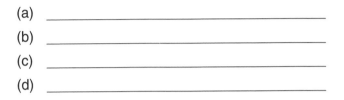

SKILLS REVIEW

EXERCISE 21-1

(a) _____

(b) _____

(c) _____

(d) _____

EXERCISE 21-2

General Journal   Page 1

		Date	Account Title	P.R.	Debit	Credit	
(a)	1						1
	2						2
	3						3
(b)	4						4
	5						5
	6						6
	7						7
(c)	8						8
	9						9
	10						10
	11						11

EXERCISE 21-3

General Journal   Page 1

		Date	Account Title	P.R.	Debit	Credit	
(a)	1						1
	2						2
	3						3
(b)	4						4
	5						5
	6						6

EXERCISE 21-4

General Journal

Page 1

	Date	Account Title	P.R.	Debit	Credit	
(a) 1						1
2						2
3						3
(b) 4						4
5						5
6						6

EXERCISE 21-5

General Journal

Page 1

	Date	Account Title	P.R.	Debit	Credit	
1						1
2						2
3						3
4						4
5						5
6						6
7						7
8						8
9						9
10						10

EXERCISE 21-6

General Journal

Page 1

	Date	Account Title	P.R.	Debit	Credit	
1						1
2						2
3						3
4						4
5						5
6						6
7						7
8						8

(a) rows 1–3, (b) rows 5–

EXERCISE 21-7

General Journal

Page 1

	Date	Account Title	P.R.	Debit	Credit	
1						1
2						2
3						3
4						4
5						5
6						6
7						7
8						8
9						9

EXERCISE 21-8

General Journal

Page 1

	Date	Account Title	P.R.	Debit	Credit	
1						1
2						2
3						3
4						4
5						5
6						6
7						7
8						8
9						9
10						10
11						11

(a) rows 1–4, (b) rows 5–7, (c) rows 8–11

EXERCISE 21-9

General Journal

		Date	Account Title	P.R.	Debit	Credit	
(a)	1						1
	2						2
	3						3
(b)	4						4
	5						5
	6						6

EXERCISE 21-10

General Journal

Page 1

	Date	Account Title	P.R.	Debit	Credit	
1						1
2						2
3						3
4						4

EXERCISE 21-11

General Journal

Page 1

		Date	Account Title	P.R.	Debit	Credit	
(a)	1						1
	2						2
	3						3
	4						4
(b)	5						5
	6						6
	7						7
	8						8

PROBLEM 21-1A OR 21-1B

General Journal   Page 1

	Date	Account Title	P.R.	Debit	Credit	
1						1
2						2
3						3
4						4
5						5
6						6
7						7
8						8
9						9
10						10
11						11
12						12
13						13
14						14
15						15
16						16
17						17
18						18
19						19
20						20
21						21
22						22
23						23
24						24
25						25
26						26
27						27
28						28
29						29
30						30
31						31
32						32

General Journal

	Date		Account Title	P.R.	Debit	Credit	
1							1
2							2
3							3
4							4
5							5
6							6
7							7
8							8
9							9
10							10
11							11
12							12
13							13
14							14
15							15
16							16
17							17
18							18
19							19
20							20
21							21
22							22
23							23
24							24
25							25
26							26
27							27
28							28
29							29
30							30
31							31
32							32

PROBLEM 21-2A OR 21-2B

General Journal

Page 1

	Date		Account Title	P.R.	Debit	Credit	
1							1
2							2
3							3
4							4
5							5
6							6
7							7
8							8
9							9
10							10
11							11
12							12
13							13
14							14
15							15
16							16
17							17
18							18
19							19
20							20
21							21
22							22
23							23
24							24
25							25
26							26
27							27
28							28
29							29
30							30
31							31
32							32

67

General Journal

	Date	Account Title	P.R.	Debit	Credit	
1						1
2						2
3						3
4						4
5						5
6						6
7						7
8						8
9						9
10						10
11						11
12						12
13						13
14						14
15						15
16						16
17						17
18						18
19						19
20						20
21						21
22						22
23						23
24						24
25						25
26						26
27						27
28						28
29						29
30						30
31						31
32						32

PROBLEM 21-3A OR 21-3A

1.

	Date		Account Title	P.R.	Debit	Credit	
1							1
2							2
3							3
4							4
5							5
6							6
7							7
8							8
9							9
10							10
11							11
12							12
13							13
14							14
15							15
16							16
17							17
18							18
19							19
20							20
21							21
22							22
23							23
24							24
25							25
26							26
27							27
28							28
29							29
30							30
31							31
32							32

General Journal

	Date		Account Title	P.R.	Debit	Credit	
1							1
2							2
3							3
4							4
5							5
6							6
7							7
8							8
9							9
10							10
11							11
12							12
13							13
14							14
15							15
16							16
17							17
18							18
19							19
20							20
21							21
22							22
23							23
24							24
25							25
26							26
27							27
28							28
29							29
30							30
31							31
32							32

2.   **GENERAL LEDGER**

ACCOUNT Interest Expense   ACCOUNT NO. 811

DATE	ITEM	P.R.	DEBIT	CREDIT	BALANCE DEBIT	BALANCE CREDIT

ACCOUNT Discount on Bonds Payable   ACCOUNT NO. 215.1

DATE	ITEM	P.R.	DEBIT	CREDIT	BALANCE DEBIT	BALANCE CREDIT

3. (a) Carrying value as of December 31, 20X1 = _____

    (b) Carrying value as of December 31, 20X2 = _____

4.

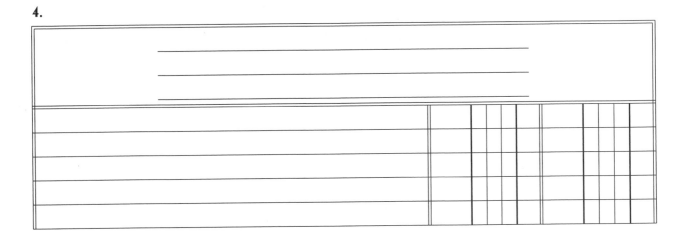

This page intentionally left blank.

General Journal

Page 1

	Date		Account Title	P.R.	Debit	Credit	
1							1
2							2
3							3
4							4
5							5
6							6
7							7
8							8
9							9
10							10
11							11
12							12
13							13
14							14
15							15
16							16
17							17
18							18
19							19
20							20
21							21
22							22
23							23
24							24
25							25
26							26
27							27
28							28
29							29
30							30
31							31
32							32

General Journal

	Date	Account Title	P.R.	Debit	Credit	
1						1
2						2
3						3
4						4
5						5
6						6
7						7
8						8
9						9
10						10
11						11
12						12
13						13
14						14
15						15
16						16
17						17
18						18
19						19
20						20
21						21
22						22
23						23
24						24
25						25
26						26
27						27
28						28
29						29
30						30
31						31
32						32

CHALLENGE PROBLEMS

PROBLEM SOLVING

PROBLEM SOLVING (continued)

COMMUNICATIONS

ETHICS

This page intentionally left blank.

PRACTICE TEST ANSWERS

PART I

1. T
2. F
3. T
4. F
5. T
6. T
7. F
8. T
9. F
10. T
11. T
12. F
13. T
14. F
15. T
16. T
17. F
18. T
19. T
20. F

PART II

1. c
2. n
3. j
4. t
5. s
6. r
7. e
8. p
9. d
10. o
11. g
12. i
13. l
14. a
15. b
16. h
17. f
18. m
19. k
20. q

PART III

1. $955
2. $1,022.50
3. Cash, Discount on Bonds Payable, Bonds Payable
4. accrued
5. amortized
6. increases
7. asset
8. current assets
9. gain, other
10. other revenue

PART IV

1. c
2. b
3. a
4. b
5. d
6. b
7. a
8. b
9. d
10. c

PART V

Answers will vary. Please discuss questions with your instructor.

WORKING PAPERS

2.

	Date		Account Title	P.R.	Debit	Credit	
1							1
2							2
3							3
4							4
5							5
6							6
7							7
8							8
9							9
10							10
11							11
12							12
13							13
14							14
15							15
16							16
17							17
18							18
19							19
20							20
21							21
22							22
23							23
24							24
25							25
26							26
27							27
28							28
29							29
30							30

General Journal — Page 25

	Date		Account Title	P.R.	Debit	Credit	
1							1
2							2
3							3
4							4
5							5
6							6
7							7
8							8
9							9
10							10
11							11
12							12
13							13
14							14
15							15
16							16
17							17
18							18
19							19
20							20
21							21
22							22
23							23
24							24
25							25
26							26
27							27
28							28
29							29
30							30
31							31
32							32

	Date		Account Title	P.R.	Debit	Credit	
1							1
2							2
3							3
4							4
5							5
6							6
7							7
8							8
9							9
10							10
11							11
12							12
13							13
14							14
15							15
16							16
17							17
18							18
19							19
20							20
21							21
22							22
23							23
24							24
25							25
26							26
27							27
28							28
29							29
30							30
31							31
32							32

1., 3.

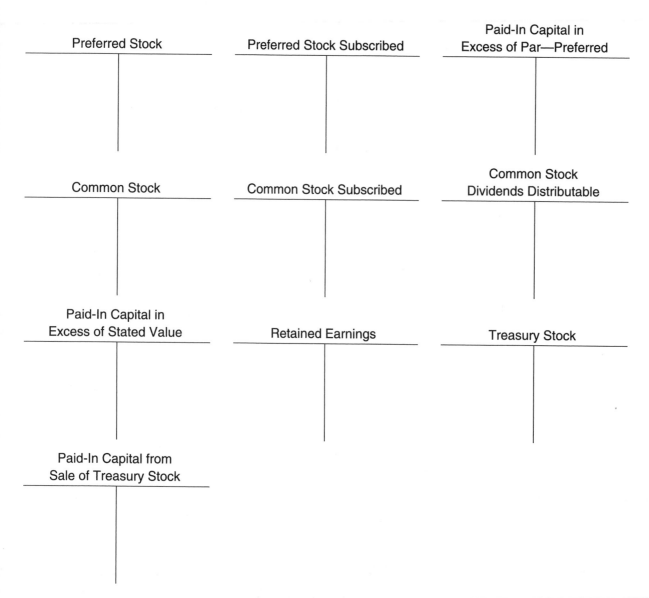

Preferred Stock

Preferred Stock Subscribed

Paid-In Capital in
Excess of Par—Preferred

Common Stock

Common Stock Subscribed

Common Stock
Dividends Distributable

Paid-In Capital in
Excess of Stated Value

Retained Earnings

Treasury Stock

Paid-In Capital from
Sale of Treasury Stock

4.

5.

Statement of Cash Flows

CHAPTER SUMMARY

In 1987, the Financial Accounting Standards Board (FASB) stated that the statement of cash flows should replace the statement of changes in financial position as the fourth required financial statement. When any financial report is published that contains both an income statement and a balance sheet, a statement of cash flows must be included.

A **statement of cash flows** has two objectives. Primarily, it reports information about the **cash flows**—cash receipts and cash payments—of a business during the period of time covered by the income statement. Secondarily, it provides information about a company's financing and investing activities.

The FASB requires that the statement of cash flows consist of three categories of activities: (1) cash flows from operating activities, (2) cash flows from investing activities, and (3) cash flows from financing activities. **Operating activities** involve transactions that enter into the calculation of net income, such as cash sales of goods and services and cash payments for inventory and expenses. **Investing activities** involve purchasing and selling long-term assets and making and collecting loans. **Financing activities** involve transactions that change long-term liabilities and stockholders' equity, such as borrowing from creditors and repaying these loans and selling stock to stockholders and paying dividends.

On a statement of cash flows, the term *cash* has a broader meaning than just currency on hand and in the bank. According to the FASB, the statement of cash flows should explain changes in cash and **cash equivalents**. A cash equivalent is a highly liquid investment, such as a short-term investment in US Treasury Bills, a money market investment, and commercial paper. These investments can be turned back into cash with little delay.

The information needed to prepare a statement of cash flows is obtained from a variety of sources. These sources include the balance sheets at the beginning and end of a period, an income statement for the period, and a retained earnings statement for the period. A comparative balance sheet is helpful when preparing a statement of cash flows because data for two or more periods are listed side by side. A combined income and retained earnings statement is also a useful tool because operating items, dividends, and changes in retained earnings are shown on one statement.

The first step in preparing a statement of cash flows is to determine how much cash has changed. This is an easy task. Simply compare the balance of the Cash account on the last day of the preceding period (the first day of the current period) with the balance of the Cash account as shown on the year-end balance sheet. The amount that cash has changed is our starting point in preparing a statement of cash flows. Using an analysis of a company's operating, investing, and financing activities, we explain why cash changed as it did.

There are two alternative methods for preparing a statement of cash flows: the direct method and the indirect method. The two methods differ only in the operating activities section; the remaining two sections—the investing activities section and the financing activities section—are the same under both methods.

The **direct method** reports details concerning sources and uses of operating cash. The **indirect method** starts out with net income and adjusts it for items that do not involve the receipt or payment of cash; that is, net income is adjusted to determine the net amount of cash from operating activities. The direct method is recommended by the FASB.

This page intentionally left blank.

PRACTICE TEST

PART I TRUE/FALSE

Please circle the correct answer.

T F 1. The income statement shows the financial position of a business at a certain date.

T F 2. The statement of owner's equity shows changes in the owner's capital account during a period.

T F 3. The balance sheet shows the assets, liabilities, and owner's equity of a business at a certain date.

T F 4. The statement of cash flows is intended primarily to provide information about the cash receipts and payments of a business during the period covered by the income statement.

T F 5. Cash is the most liquid asset of a business and the most important asset.

T F 6. Investing activities include sale of the company's stock.

T F 7. The first step in preparing a statement of cash flows is to calculate the cash flows from operating activities.

T F 8. To prepare a statement of cash flows, information is needed from a comparative balance sheet, an income statement, and a retained earnings statement.

T F 9. The operating activities of a business include the sale of old plant assets.

T F 10. The financing activities of a business include the payment of interest on the debts of the company.

T F 11. To calculate the cash inflow from customers, take the beginning balance of Accounts Receivable, add the sales revenue, and subtract the ending balance of Accounts Receivable.

T F 12. Depreciation is considered an inflow of cash.

T F 13. An accrued liability means that an expense has been recognized that has not yet been paid with cash.

T F 14. A prepaid expense means that cash has been paid for an expense that has not yet been recognized.

T F 15. The investing activities of a business include collecting cash when the principal of a loan is paid to the business.

T F 16. If a company borrows money by issuing bonds, that money is considered a cash inflow from financing activities.

T F 17. The purchase of treasury stock is a financing activity.

T F 18. The payment of dividends to stockholders is an investing activity.

T F 19. The indirect method of computing the cash flows from operating activities is recommended by the FASB.

T F 20. The statement of cash flows is an optional statement.

PART II MATCHING

Please match each of the following terms with its definition.

a. balance sheet
b. cash equivalent
c. financing activities
d. income statement
e. investing activities
f. operating activities
g. retained earnings statement
h. statement of cash flows
i. statement of changes in financial position
j. statement of owner's equity

_____ 1. A financial statement that summarizes the amount of revenue and expenses for a specific period of time and reports the results of operations.

_____ 2. A financial statement that summarizes the changes that have occurred in retained earnings over a specific period of time.

_____ 3. A financial statement that shows the assets, liabilities, and owner's equity of a business as of a certain date.

_____ 4. A financial statement that summarizes the changes that have occurred in the owner's capital account during a period.

_____ 5. A financial statement that provides information about the cash receipts and cash payments of a business during a period.

_____ 6. A financial statement that was required by the FASB prior to its replacement by the statement of cash flows.

_____ 7. Transactions that enter into the calculation of net income.

_____ 8. Transactions that involve the purchase and sale of long-term assets and transactions that involve making and collecting loans.

_____ 9. Transactions that involve cash receipts or payments from changes in long-term liabilities and stockholders' equity.

_____ 10. A highly liquid short-term investment that can easily be converted to cash.

PART III FILL IN THE BLANKS

Please complete each sentence with the correct word or words.

1. Cash is a company's most _____ asset.

2. The statement of _____ shows much more about cash than other financial statements.

3. The statement of cash flows allows users to observe the _____ for the changes in the company's cash balance.

4. The statement of cash flows helps users judge the company's ability to pay its _____ and to pay _____ to shareholders.

5. The statement of cash flows helps users to assess the company's need to _____ money.

6. The first step in the preparation of a statement of cash flows is to determine how much _____ has changed.

7. Depreciation is considered neither a(n) _____ nor a(n) _____ of cash.

8. Cash paid for interest can be computed by taking interest expense and adding any _____ in interest payable or subtracting any _____ in interest payable.

9. Sale of a plant asset will result in a(n) _____ of cash from _____ activities.

10. _____ paid to shareholders is a financing activity.

11. The statement of cash flows has _____ sections.

12. The ending balance of _____ must be shown on the statement of cash flows.

13. The _____ method differs from the direct method only in its presentation of the cash flows from operating activities.

14. The _____ method is recommended by the FASB.

15. The statement of cash flows replaced the statement of changes in _____.

PART IV MULTIPLE CHOICE

Please circle the correct answer.

1. Issuing common stock is classified as
   a. an operating activity.
   b. an investing activity.
   c. a financing activity.
   d. none of the above.

2. Paying suppliers for inventory is classified as
   a. an operating activity.
   b. an investing activity.
   c. a financing activity.
   d. none of the above.

3. Purchasing plant assets is classified as
   a. an operating activity.
   b. an investing activity.
   c. a financing activity.
   d. none of the above.

4. Collecting cash on account from credit customers is classified as
   a. an operating activity.
   b. an investing activity.
   c. a financing activity.
   d. none of the above.

5. Issuing common stock as payment for a new building is classified as
   a. an operating activity.
   b. an investing activity.
   c. a financing activity.
   d. none of the above.

6. Purchasing the stocks and bonds of other companies is classified as
   a. an operating activity.
   b. an investing activity.
   c. a financing activity.
   d. none of the above.

7. Paying income taxes is classified as
   a. an operating activity.
   b. an investing activity.
   c. a financing activity.
   d. none of the above.

8. Collecting cash for the principal of loans made to others is classified as
   a. an operating activity.
   b. an investing activity.
   c. a financing activity.
   d. none of the above.

9. Paying interest on a loan owed by the business is classified as
   a. an operating activity.
   b. an investing activity.
   c. a financing activity.
   d. none of the above.

10. Purchasing government bonds is classified as
    a. an operating activity.
    b. an investing activity.
    c. a financing activity.
    d. none of the above.

PART V WRITING/SHORT ANSWER

1. **Reflect** Make a list, in words or simple phrases, of the most important and meaningful points in this chapter.

2. **Question** Think about the most confusing points or the material you do not understand in this chapter. Write down two or three questions that remain unanswered.

3. **Connect** Explain, in one or two sentences, the connection between the main points of this chapter and the major goals of the entire course.

4. **Summarize** Review this chapter's Joining the Pieces visual summary and explain the concept(s) illustrated in a few sentences.

WORKING PAPERS

SKILLS REVIEW

EXERCISE 22-1

(a) Cash received from customers = _____

(b) Cash received from customers = _____

EXERCISE 22-2

_____

_____

_____

_____

_____

Cash paid for inventory = _____

EXERCISE 22-3

(a) _____

(b) _____

(c) _____

_____

EXERCISE 22-4

Amount of cash paid for income tax = _____

EXERCISE 22-5

_____

_____

_____

_____

_____

EXERCISE 22-6

_____

_____

_____

EXERCISE 22-7

EXERCISE 22-8

CASE PROBLEMS

PROBLEM 22-1A OR 22-1B

This page intentionally left blank.

This page intentionally left blank.

This page intentionally left blank.

PROBLEM 22-4A OR 22-4B

This page intentionally left blank.

This page intentionally left blank.

CHALLENGE PROBLEMS

PROBLEM SOLVING

This page intentionally left blank.

COMMUNICATIONS

_____

_____

_____

_____

_____

_____

_____

_____

_____

_____

_____

_____

_____

_____

_____

ETHICS

_____

_____

_____

_____

_____

_____

_____

_____

_____

_____

_____

_____

_____

_____

_____

_____

_____

This page intentionally left blank.

PRACTICE TEST ANSWERS

PART I

1. F
2. T
3. T
4. T
5. T
6. F
7. F
8. T
9. F
10. F
11. T
12. F
13. T
14. T
15. T
16. T
17. T
18. F
19. F
20. F

PART II

1. d
2. g
3. a
4. j
5. h
6. i
7. f
8. e
9. c
10. b

PART III

1. liquid
2. cash flows

3. reasons
4. debts, dividends
5. borrow
6. cash
7. inflow, outflow
8. decrease, increase
9. inflow, investing
10. Dividends
11. three
12. cash
13. indirect
14. direct
15. financial position

PART IV

1. c
2. a
3. b
4. a
5. d
6. b
7. a
8. b
9. a
10. b

PART V

Answers will vary. Please discuss questions with your instructor.

Analysis and Interpretation of Financial Statements

CHAPTER SUMMARY

The preparation of financial statements is a basic step in the process of accounting. A vital later step is analyzing the financial statements in order to observe the progress, either positive or negative, of a business. The tools we use to analyze financial statements include vertical analysis, horizontal analysis, liquidity analysis, and profitability analysis. These methods permit the analysis of a company's performance and financial position over time, which is more useful than observing only one year's financial statements.

Horizontal analysis uses **comparative financial statements** to compare each item on a financial statement with the same item from a previous accounting period or periods. With this method, we compare the dollar difference and compute a percentage difference using the earliest year in the analysis as the base year. The percentages help identify favorable and unfavorable changes in financial statement items.

Vertical analysis, as the name implies, looks at the financial statements from top to bottom. On the income statement, items are calculated as a percentage of net sales. On the balance sheet, percentages are calculated based on total assets. As is the case with horizontal analysis, two or more years of statements with vertical percentages are useful in identifying changes, observing trends, and spotting problem areas.

Trend percentages are calculated by choosing a time frame (for example, five years), selecting a base year as 100%, and expressing all items selected for the analysis as percentages of the base year items. This analysis allows a percentage comparison of financial statement items covering several accounting periods.

Liquidity analysis and **profitability analysis** usually use **ratios** to compare financial position and performance. Liquidity and profitability measures provide analysts with a variety of indicators that may be used to evaluate a business based on its own previous ratios and also the ratios of other businesses. The financial ratios may be categorized as follows:

A. Liquidity analysis

    1. Short-term liquidity

        Measures: **Working capital**
                   Current ratio
                   Acid-test (quick) ratio
                   Accounts receivable turnover
                   Average collection period for accounts receivable
                   Merchandise inventory turnover
                   Number of days in merchandise inventory

    2. Long-term liquidity

        Measures: **Ratio of plant assets to long-term liabilities**
                   Ratio of owner's equity to total liabilities
                   Times interest earned

B. Profitability analysis

    Measures: **Return on total assets**
                  Asset turnover
                  Return on stockholders' equity
                  Earnings per share on common stock
                  Price/earnings (P/E) ratio
                  Dividend yield

PRACTICE TEST

PART I TRUE/FALSE

Please circle the correct answer.

T   F   1. Accounting is defined as the process of recording, summarizing, analyzing, and interpreting financial activities to permit individuals and organizations to make informed judgments and decisions.

T   F   2. In order to know whether a company is doing better or worse this year than last year, it is necessary to have comparative financial statements.

T   F   3. In horizontal analysis, each item in a company's financial statements is compared to some specific base figure.

T   F   4. Net income of 12.5% of net sales this year and 14.1% of net sales last year indicates a favorable change.

T   F   5. Trend percentages are used to compare financial data covering a period of years.

T   F   6. Liquidity analysis measures a firm's ability to earn a profit.

T   F   7. The current ratio is a measure of profitability.

T   F   8. The acid-test ratio is a comparison of current liabilities and quick assets (cash, current receivables, and marketable securities).

T   F   9. An acid-test ratio of 1 to 1 is an indication that a company has a strong short-term credit position.

T   F   10. Accounts receivable turnover measures how many accounts must be turned over to a collection agent.

T   F   11. If the average collection period for accounts receivable is 65 days and the company offers credit terms of 2/10,n/30, the company is doing a good job of collecting its receivables.

T   F   12. Inventory turnover measures the number of times a company's inventory is sold each year.

T   F   13. A ratio of 2 to 1 is considered good when measuring the ratio of plant assets to long-term liabilities.

T   F   14. Creditors think that a company that is heavily financed is a good investment because so many other creditors have put money in it.

T   F   15. Profitability refers to the ability of a company to earn a reasonable return on the investment in the business.

T   F   16. Profitability measures include inventory turnover and times interest earned.

T   F   17. The return on total assets is like the interest rate on a savings account—it is the rate of return being earned on the company's investment in assets.

T   F   18. Earnings per share is the same as the dividend per share.

T   F   19. Financial statement analysis allows the user of financial statements to "read between the lines" and see more than just the numbers alone.

T   F   20. Good financial statement analysis can aid the user in making good financial decisions.

PART II MATCHING

Please match each of the following terms with its definition.

a. base year
b. comparative financial statements
c. current assets
d. current liabilities
e. horizontal analysis

f. liquidity
g. profitability
h. quick assets
i. trend percentages
j. vertical analysis

_____ 1. Cash and assets that will be consumed or converted into cash in the course of one year or less.

_____ 2. Financial statements that provide information for two or more periods.

_____ 3. The comparison of each item in a company's financial statements with that same item from a previous accounting period or periods in order to find the dollar difference and the percentage difference.

_____ 4. The ability of a business to earn a reasonable return on the owners' investments.

_____ 5. The year against which all other years are compared.

_____ 6. Measures used to compare financial data covering a period of years in order to observe the direction of changes.

_____ 7. Debts that are to be paid within one year using current assets.

_____ 8. The expression of each item on a financial statement as a percentage of a specific base figure.

_____ 9. Cash, marketable securities, and current receivables; assets that can be quickly converted to cash.

_____ 10. The ability of a business to pay its debts as they come due.

PART III FILL IN THE BLANKS

Please complete each sentence with the correct word or words.

1. For financial statements to be of greatest benefit, certain _____ and _____ must be made.

2. The purpose of financial statement analysis is to assist the user to make good _____ and _____.

3. Horizontal analysis compares each item on a company's financial statements with that _____ from a previous accounting period or periods.

4. Vertical analysis compares each item from a single accounting period with a specific _____ figure.

5. The use of _____ percentages is helpful in analyzing data from several years.

6. The current ratio is computed by dividing _____ by _____.

7. The _____ ratio is computed by dividing quick assets by current liabilities.

8. A general rule is that the current ratio should be at least _____.

9. Accounts receivable turnover indicates how quickly a company is _____ its accounts receivable.

10. _____ is computed by dividing net credit sales by average net accounts receivable.

11. The average collection period for accounts receivable shows how well a company is enforcing its _____ policy.

12. Merchandise inventory turnover is computed by dividing the _____ by the average inventory.

13. It is important for a company to sell its inventory rapidly to avoid losses from _____ and _____ goods.

14. Potential lenders would be interested in a company's ratio of owner's equity to _____.

15. The calculation of times interest earned gives an indication of a company's ability to make its _____.

16. _____ refers to the ability of a company to earn a reasonable return on the investment in the business.

17. Profitability measures include return on total assets, return on stockholders' equity, and _____.

18. Earnings per share and return on stockholders' equity focus on the return on _____ investments.

19. Earnings per share is calculated by dividing _____ by the number of common shares outstanding.

20. Ordinarily, the _____ number of common shares outstanding will be used to calculate earnings per share when more stock is being issued by the company or when stock is reacquired.

PART IV MULTIPLE CHOICE

Please circle the correct answer.

1. Accounting includes which of the following functions?
   a. recording and summarizing
   b. analyzing
   c. interpreting
   d. all of the above

2. A horizontal analysis is done by
   a. subtracting the amount for the base year from the amount for the current year and dividing by the amount for the base year.
   b. subtracting the amount for the current year from the amount for the base year and dividing by the amount for the base year.
   c. adding the amount for the current year to the amount for the base year and dividing by two.
   d. none of the above.

3. The purpose of a vertical analysis is
   a. to see the relative importance of each item on the financial statements.
   b. to compare the percentages from one year to the next.
   c. to identify favorable and unfavorable changes in the percentages.
   d. all of the above.

4. Measures of short-term liquidity include the
   a. earnings per share.
   b. current ratio.
   c. ratio of plant assets to long-term liabilities.
   d. return on stockholders' equity.

5. Measures of long-term liquidity include the
   a. earnings per share.
   b. current ratio.
   c. ratio of plant assets to long-term liabilities.
   d. return on stockholders' equity.

6. Profitability measures include the
   a. times interest earned.
   b. acid-test ratio.
   c. earnings per share.
   d. accounts receivable turnover.

7. The number of days' sales in merchandise inventory is computed by dividing 365 by the
   a. net sales.
   b. inventory turnover rate.
   c. average inventory.
   d. cost of goods sold.

8. The accounts receivable turnover and the average collection period for accounts receivable are measures of
   a. how well the company carries out its credit policy.
   b. how good the economy is.
   c. how well the credit department screens its credit customers.
   d. all of the above.

9. A steadily increasing percentage of cost of goods sold could indicate
   a. that the costs of inventory are going up more slowly than selling prices.
   b. that the costs of inventory are going up faster than selling prices.
   c. that too much inventory is on hand.
   d. none of the above.

10. The ratio of plant assets to long-term liabilities indicates
    a. how many dollars of long-term debt there are to each dollar of plant assets.
    b. the rate of return on investment in plant assets.
    c. the number of plant assets mortgaged to the bondholders.
    d. none of the above.

PART V WRITING/SHORT ANSWER

1. **Reflect** Make a list, in words or simple phrases, of the most important and meaningful points in this chapter.

2. **Question** Think about the most confusing points or the material you do not understand in this chapter. Write down two or three questions that remain unanswered.

3. **Connect** Explain, in one or two sentences, the connection between the main points of this chapter and the major goals of the entire course.

4. **Summarize** Review this chapter's Joining the Pieces visual summary and explain the concept(s) illustrated in a few sentences.

SKILLS REVIEW

EXERCISE 23-1

	Amount	Percent
(a)		
(b)		
(c)		
(d)		
(e)		
(f)		
(g)		

EXERCISE 23-2

	Amount	Percent

EXERCISE 23-3

	Amount	Percent

EXERCISE 23-4

	20X0	20X1	20X2	20X3	20X4
Net sales					
Trend percentage					

EXERCISE 23-5

(a) Working capital

(b) Current ratio

(c) Acid-test ratio

EXERCISE 23-6

(a)

(b)

(c)

EXERCISE 23-7

(a)

(b)

(c)

EXERCISE 23-8

(a)

(b)

(c)

CASE PROBLEMS

PROBLEM 23-1A OR 23-1B

1.

			Increase or (Decrease)	
			Amount	Percent

2.

1.

	Amount	Percent	Amount	Percent

2.
_____

_____

_____

_____

_____

_____

_____

_____

_____

_____

_____

_____

_____

_____

_____

_____

_____

_____

PROBLEM 23-3A OR 23-3B

(a) Working capital =

(b) Current ratio =

(c) Acid-test ratio =

(d) Accounts receivable turnover =

(e) Average collection period for accounts receivable =

(f) Merchandise inventory turnover =

(g) Number of days in inventory =

(h) Ratio of plant assets to long-term liabilities =

(i) Ratio of owner's equity to total liabilities =

(j) Times interest earned =

This page intentionally left blank.

PROBLEM 23-4A OR 23-4B

(a) Return on total assets =

(b) Asset turnover =

(c) Return on stockholders' equity =

(d) Earnings per share on common stock =

(e) Price/earnings ratio =

(f) Dividend yield =

This page intentionally left blank.

CHALLENGE PROBLEMS

PROBLEM SOLVING

Liquidity Measures	20X3	20X2
(1) Working capital		
(2) Current ratio		
(3) Acid-test ratio		
(4) Accounts receivable turnover		
(5) Average collection period for accounts receivable		
(6) Merchandise inventory turnover		
(7) Number of days in inventory		
(8) Ratio of plant assets to long-term liabilities		
(9) Ratio of owner's equity to total liabilities		
(10) Times interest earned		

Profitability Measures		
(11) Return on total assets		
(12) Asset turnover		
(13) Return on stockholders' equity		
(14) Earnings per share on common stock		
(15) Price/earnings ratio		
(16) Dividend yield		

PROBLEM SOLVING (continued)

Comments: _____

_____

_____

_____

_____

_____

_____

_____

_____

_____

_____

_____

_____

_____

_____

_____

_____

_____

COMMUNICATIONS

ETHICS

This page intentionally left blank.

PRACTICE TEST ANSWERS

PART I

1. T
2. T
3. F
4. F
5. T
6. F
7. F
8. T
9. T
10. F
11. F
12. T
13. T
14. F
15. T
16. F
17. T
18. F
19. T
20. T

PART II

1. c
2. b
3. e
4. g
5. a
6. i
7. d
8. j
9. h
10. f

PART III

1. analyses, comparisons
2. judgments, decisions

3. same item
4. base
5. trend
6. current assets, current liabilities
7. acid-test
8. 2 to 1
9. collecting
10. Accounts receivable turnover
11. credit
12. cost of goods sold
13. spoiled, obsolete
14. total liabilities
15. interest payments
16. Profitability
17. earnings per share
18. stockholders'
19. net income
20. average

PART IV

1. d
2. a
3. d
4. b
5. c
6. c
7. b
8. d
9. b
10. a

PART V

Answers will vary. Please discuss questions with your instructor.

Accounting for Departments and Branches

CHAPTER SUMMARY

A firm that uses **responsibility accounting** breaks down an organization into parts in order to hold those in charge of each part responsible for the efficiency of that part. The division of an organization into parts is called **segmentation**. Segments may be departments, branches, products, geographic regions, foreign versus domestic, or **profit centers** (segments that incur expenses while producing revenue).

Segmentation of an income statement by department can be done through gross profit, through net operating income, or through department margin. To segment through gross profit, it is necessary to determine sales and cost of goods sold by department. Thus, sales, purchases, and inventory are recorded separately for each department. Then, an income statement segmented through gross profit is prepared.

To segment through net operating income, an additional step is required: **apportionment** of operating expenses between (or among) departments. The process of apportionment is based on fair and reasonable assumptions about how expenses should be divided. Examples shown in the chapter are summarized as follows:

Expense	Basis for Apportionment
sales salaries	department records
advertising	space or time used by department in advertisements
uncollectible accounts	percent of sales
depreciation—store equipment	actual value in department
repairs	actual records
store supplies	department sales
office salaries	time devoted to departments
rent	square footage
depreciation—office equipment	time used for departments
insurance—property	value of assets in department
insurance—liability and casualty	department sales
office supplies	time devoted to departments
utilities	square footage

To calculate the real value of a department to the business as a whole, a procedure called **departmental margin analysis** is carried out. The **departmental margin** is gross profit less direct expenses. A **direct expense** is an expense that benefits only a single department. If the department did not exist, the direct expense would not exist. An **indirect expense** is one that is not traceable to a specific department, one that would continue even if the department were not there. If a department with a positive departmental margin were discontinued, the net income of the firm would decrease by the amount of that margin.

Branch accounting systems can be centralized or decentralized. In a **centralized branch accounting system**, the **home office** (main location) keeps all records. In a **decentralized branch accounting system**, separate records are kept by the home office and the branches.

In a decentralized system, the branch has no owner's equity account but instead keeps an account entitled Home Office. The home office maintains an account with an equal but opposite balance called **Branch**. These two accounts are **reciprocal accounts**, accounts that match in dollar amount but have opposite balances. Shipments from Home Office (branch books) and Shipments to Branch (home office books) are also reciprocal accounts.

Most entries in the branch books are routine. However, any interaction with the home office requires the use of reciprocal accounts. When the home office ships merchandise to the branch, the following entries are made:

BRANCH BOOKS	HOME OFFICE BOOKS
Shipments from Home Office	Branch
Home Office	Shipments to Branch

Standard adjusting and closing entries are made in the branch books. The Shipments from Home Office account is closed to the Income Summary account. The Income Summary account is closed to the Home Office account, requiring an entry on the home office books. To record branch net income:

BRANCH BOOKS	HOME OFFICE BOOKS
Income Summary	Branch
Home Office	Branch Net Income

On a branch income statement, the Shipments from Home Office account assumes the usual place of Purchases. On a branch balance sheet, the Home Office account replaces owner's equity. On a home office income statement, the Shipments to Branch account is added to Sales. On a home office balance sheet, the Branch account is listed as an asset. On combined home office-branch statements, no reciprocal accounts appear.

PRACTICE TEST

PART I TRUE/FALSE

Please circle the correct answer.

T F 1. Departments and branches are segments of a business.

T F 2. Dividing a business into departments and accounting for the profitability of each department is one way of holding managers responsible for the operation of their departments.

T F 3. A profit center is a segment of a firm that produces revenue but has no expenses.

T F 4. Some departments in a business may not produce any revenue.

T F 5. A company that reports gross profit by departments must have separate records for sales and operating expenses.

T F 6. Operating expenses are always easy to trace directly to the individual departments.

T F 7. Apportionment of operating expenses must be done in some reasonable and fair manner.

T F 8. Departmental margin analysis is the determination of the actual contribution of a specific department to the profitability of a firm.

T F 9. The departmental margin is gross profit minus all expenses apportioned to the department.

T F 10. Sometimes a department looks as if it is losing money, but if all indirect expenses are eliminated from the calculation, the department may be making a positive contribution to company profit.

T F 11. In centralized branch accounting, each branch keeps its own records and prepares its own financial statements.

T F 12. The books of a branch will have certain accounts that are offset by similar accounts on the books of the home office.

T F 13. Adjusting entries on branch books differ from those on other sets of books.

T F 14. Branch books contain an account called Home Office in place of an account for owner's equity.

T F 15. When the financial statements of a branch are combined with those of the home office, all the reciprocal accounts are omitted.

PART II MATCHING

Please match each of the following terms with its definition.

a. apportionment
b. departmental margin
c. departmental margin analysis
d. direct expense
e. home office

f. indirect expense
g. profit centers
h. reciprocal accounts
i. responsibility accounting
j. segmentation

_____ 1. A management tool that holds those in charge of each part of an organization responsible for the efficiency of that part.

_____ 2. The determination of the actual financial contribution of a specific department to a firm.

_____ 3. The division of an organization into parts.

_____ 4. The division of operating expenses among the various departments.

_____ 5. An expense that is not directly traceable to a department and that would continue if the department were eliminated.

_____ 6. The main location of a company.

_____ 7. Gross profit of a department less the direct expenses of that department.

_____ 8. An expense that benefits only a single department.

_____ 9. Accounts on both the branch and home office books that have equal dollar amounts and opposite balances.

_____ 10. Segments of a business that incur expenses while producing revenue.

PART III FILL IN THE BLANKS

Please complete each sentence with the correct word or words.

1. _____ accounting breaks down an organization into parts and accounts for the profitability of each part so that the people in charge of each part can be held responsible for the part's success or failure.

2. One form of _____ is keeping records by department.

3. Segmentation by _____ could be done by a firm with operations in all parts of the United States.

4. A profit center differs from a department in that a department does not always produce _____.

5. Accounting by departments through gross profit requires that records be kept by department for _____ and _____.

6. Accounting by departments through net operating income requires that some operating expenses be _____ to the departments.

7. Apportionment of expenses should be both _____ and _____.

8. Departmental margin is the _____ of a department minus its _____ expenses.

9. The _____ represents the real loss to a company from eliminating a department.

10. Accounting for a branch is virtually _____ to accounting for any other operation except that the branch has no _____ account.

11. The _____ account on the branch books serves as the owner's equity account for the branch.

12. The _____ account on the books of the home office acts as a _____ from the branch.

13. Transactions between the home office and the branch must be entered on _____ set(s) of books.

14. In a(n) _____ branch accounting system, the home office maintains all accounting records.

15. On the combined financial statements of the home office and the branch, all _____ accounts are eliminated.

PART IV MULTIPLE CHOICE

Please circle the correct answer.

1. The types of segmentation in which operations are broken down by location are
   a. foreign and domestic.
   b. geographic region.
   c. product.
   d. both a and b above.

2. Any form of segmentation requires
   a. that the segments be located in different places.
   b. that the segments deal in the same product.
   c. that accounting records be kept for each segment.
   d. none of the above.

3. A profit center differs from a department in that
   a. a profit center is bigger than a department.
   b. a profit center produces revenue and a department does not always do so.
   c. a profit center produces revenue and a department incurs expenses.
   d. there is no difference between a department and a profit center.

4. Gross profit calculation by department requires that departmental records be kept for
   a. sales, cost of goods sold, and operating expenses.
   b. cost of goods sold and operating expenses.
   c. sales and cost of goods sold.
   d. sales and operating expenses.

5. When departmental margin is calculated,
   a. direct expenses are subtracted from gross profit.
   b. operating expenses are subtracted from gross profit.
   c. indirect expenses are subtracted from gross profit.
   d. gross profit and departmental margin are the same.

6. Calculating net operating income by departments requires that
   a. all operating and nonoperating expenses be apportioned to the departments.
   b. all operating expenses be apportioned to the departments.
   c. all indirect expenses be apportioned to the departments.
   d. all direct expenses be apportioned to the departments.

7. Shipment of merchandise to a branch requires the following entry on the books of the branch:
   a. a debit to Shipments from Home Office and a credit to Home Office.
   b. a debit to Purchases and a credit to Home Office.
   c. a debit to Purchases and a credit to Home Office Payable.
   d. a debit to Merchandise Inventory and a credit to Accounts Payable.

8. The Income Summary account for a branch is closed to
   a. the owner's capital account.
   b. the Retained Earnings account.
   c. the Home Office account.
   d. none of the above.

9. When the home office ships merchandise to the branch, the following entry is required on the home office books:
   a. a debit to Merchandise Inventory and a credit to Accounts Payable.
   b. a debit to Branch and a credit to Shipments to Branch.
   c. a debit to Accounts Receivable and a credit to Sales.
   d. none of the above.

10. Net income from the branch is recorded on the home office books by
    a. debiting Accounts Payable and crediting Cash.
    b. debiting Accounts Receivable and crediting Sales.
    c. debiting Branch and crediting Branch Net Income.
    d. debiting Branch and crediting Other Revenue.

PART V WRITING/SHORT ANSWER

1. **Reflect** Make a list, in words or simple phrases, of the most important and meaningful points in this chapter.

2. **Question** Think about the most confusing points or the material you do not understand in this chapter. Write down two or three questions that remain unanswered.

3. **Connect** Explain, in one or two sentences, the connection between the main points of this chapter and the major goals of the entire course.

4. **Summarize** Review this chapter's Joining the Pieces visual summary and explain the concept(s) illustrated in a few sentences.

WORKING PAPERS

SKILL REVIEW

EXERCISE 24-1

Sales Journal   Page 12

Date	Inv. No.	Account Debited	P.R.	Accounts Receivable Debit	Sales Dept. A Credit	Sales Dept. B Credit	Sales Dept. C Credit

General Ledger

ACCOUNT **Accounts Receivable**   ACCOUNT NO. 112

DATE	ITEM	P.R.	DEBIT	CREDIT	BALANCE DEBIT	BALANCE CREDIT

ACCOUNT **Sales—Dept. A**   ACCOUNT NO. 411

DATE	ITEM	P.R.	DEBIT	CREDIT	BALANCE DEBIT	BALANCE CREDIT

ACCOUNT **Sales—Dept. B**   ACCOUNT NO. 412

DATE	ITEM	P.R.	DEBIT	CREDIT	BALANCE DEBIT	BALANCE CREDIT

EXERCISE 24-1 (continued)

ACCOUNT Sales—Dept. C   ACCOUNT NO. 413

DATE	ITEM	P.R.	DEBIT	CREDIT	BALANCE DEBIT	BALANCE CREDIT

EXERCISE 24-2

Department	Column Inches	% of Total	Minutes	% of Total
A				
B				
C				

Media Ads _____

Dept. A: _____

Dept. B: _____

Dept. C: _____

_____

Newspaper Ads _____

Dept. A: _____

Dept. B: _____

Dept. C: _____

_____

Total Advertising Expense

Dept. A: _____

Dept. B: _____

Dept. C: _____

_____

EXERCISE 24-3

Department	Sales	% of Total
A	_____	
B	_____	
C	_____	
D	_____	
	_____	

(a) Uncollectible accounts expense

Dept. A: _____

Dept. B: _____

Dept. C: _____

Dept. D: _____

_____

(b) Store supplies expense

Dept. A: _____

Dept. B: _____

Dept. C: _____

Dept. D: _____

_____

(c) Liability insurance expense

Dept. A: _____

Dept. B: _____

Dept. C: _____

Dept. D: _____

_____

EXERCISE 24-4

Department	Square Feet	% of Total
A	_____	
B	_____	
C	_____	
	_____	

(a) Rent expense

Dept. A: _____

Dept. B: _____

Dept. C: _____

_____

(b) Utilities expense

Dept. A: _____

Dept. B: _____

Dept. C: _____

_____

EXERCISE 24-5

(a)

Toy Department													

(b)

Toy Department													

(c) _____

_____

_____

_____

EXERCISE 24-6

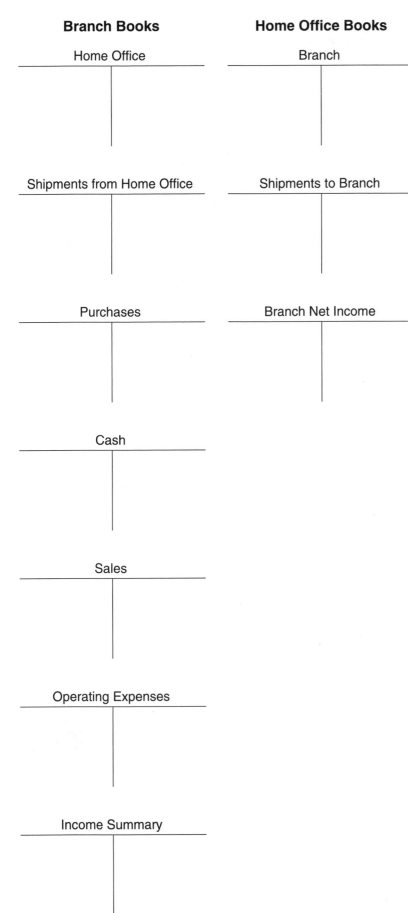

Branch Books

Home Office

Shipments from Home Office

Purchases

Cash

Sales

Operating Expenses

Income Summary

Home Office Books

Branch

Shipments to Branch

Branch Net Income

EXERCISE 24-7

Branch Books   **General Journal**   Page 1

	Date	Account Title	P.R.	Debit	Credit	
1						1
2						2
3						3
4						4
5						5
6						6
7						7
8						8
9						9
10						10
11						11
12						12
13						13

Home Office Books   **General Journal**   Page 1

	Date	Account Title	P.R.	Debit	Credit	
1						1
2						2
3						3
4						4
5						5

CASE PROBLEMS

PROBLEM 24-1A OR 24-1B

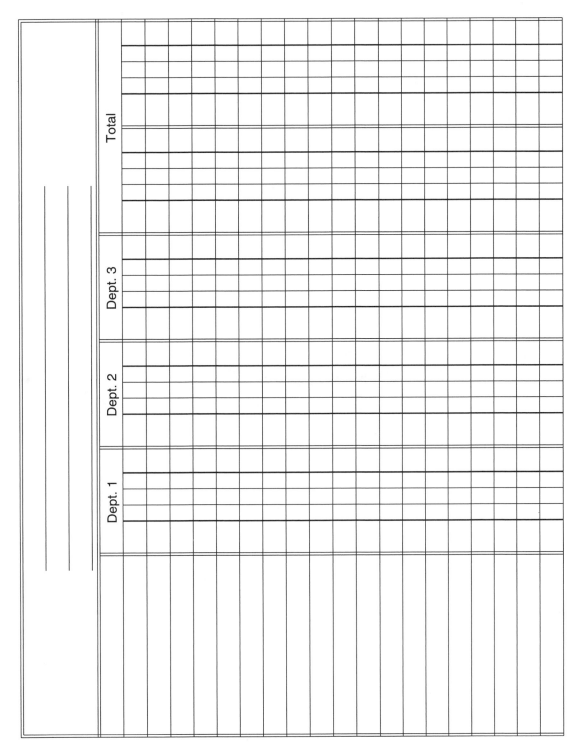

This page intentionally left blank.

This page intentionally left blank.

PROBLEM 24-2A OR 24-2B

(Left side)

	Department ____	Department ____

(Right side)

	Department ____		Total	

This page intentionally left blank.

This page intentionally left blank.

PROBLEM 24-3A OR 24-3B

(Left side)

	Department ____												Department ____											

Based on net sales: sales salaries; uncollectible accounts; store supplies

_____

_____

_____

Based on equipment value: repairs; depr.—store; insurance

_____

_____

_____

PROBLEM 24-3A OR 24-3B (continued)

	Department _____		Total

Based on area: rent; utilities

_____

_____

_____

Based on office time devoted: office salaries; depr.—office; office supplies

_____

_____

_____

This page intentionally left blank.

PROBLEM 24-4A OR 24-4B

_____ Department																					

Comments: _____

_____

_____

_____

This page intentionally left blank.

PROBLEM 24-5A OR 24-5B

1.

Branch Books **General Journal** Page 1

	Date	Account Title	P.R.	Debit	Credit	
1						1
2						2
3						3
4						4
5						5
6						6
7						7
8						8
9						9
10						10
11						11
12						12
13						13
14						14
15						15
16						16
17						17
18						18
19						19
20						20
21						21
22						22
23						23
24						24
25						25
26						26
27						27
28						28
29						29
30						30
31						31
32						32

2.

Home Office Books   **General Journal**   Page 1

	Date	Account Title	P.R.	Debit	Credit	
1						1
2						2
3						3
4						4
5						5
6						6
7						7
8						8
9						9
10						10
11						11
12						12

3.

Branch Books   **General Ledger**

ACCOUNT Home Office   ACCOUNT NO. 321

DATE	ITEM	P.R.	DEBIT	CREDIT	BALANCE	
					DEBIT	CREDIT

ACCOUNT Shipments from Home Office   ACCOUNT NO. 521

DATE	ITEM	P.R.	DEBIT	CREDIT	BALANCE	
					DEBIT	CREDIT

Home Office Books   **General Ledger**

ACCOUNT Branch   ACCOUNT NO. 131

DATE	ITEM	P.R.	DEBIT	CREDIT	BALANCE DEBIT	BALANCE CREDIT

ACCOUNT Shipments to Branch   ACCOUNT NO. 319

DATE	ITEM	P.R.	DEBIT	CREDIT	BALANCE DEBIT	BALANCE CREDIT

This page intentionally left blank.

1., 2.   **General Journal**   Page 1

	Date	Account Title	P.R.	Debit	Credit	
1						1
2						2
3						3
4						4
5						5
6						6
7						7
8						8
9						9
10						10
11						11
12						12
13						13
14						14
15						15
16						16
17						17
18						18
19						19
20						20
21						21
22						22
23						23
24						24
25						25
26						26
27						27
28						28
29						29
30						30
31						31
32						32

3.

4.

This page intentionally left blank.

CHALLENGE PROBLEMS

PROBLEM SOLVING

(a), (b)

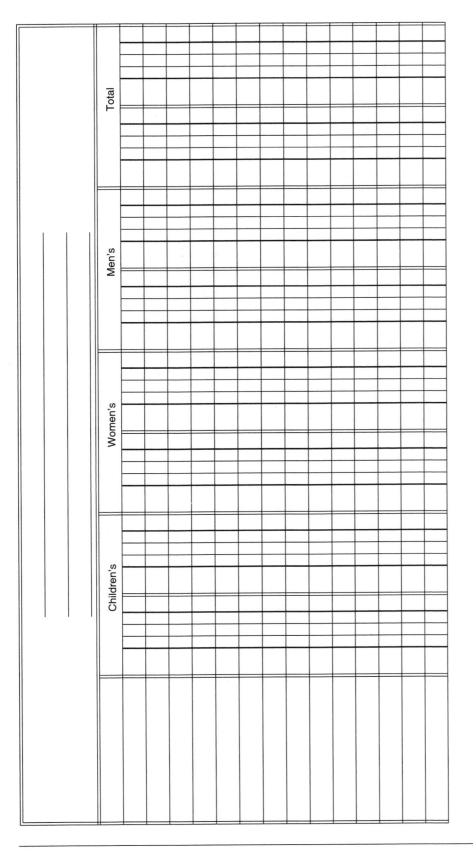

PROBLEM SOLVING (continued)

(c)

	Children's	Women's	Men's	Total

(d)

	Children's	Women's	Total

Comments: _____

_____

_____

_____

_____

_____

_____

_____

_____

_____

_____

_____

_____

_____

_____

_____

_____

_____

_____

This page intentionally left blank.

COMMUNICATIONS

_____

_____

_____

_____

_____

_____

_____

_____

_____

_____

_____

_____

_____

_____

_____

ETHICS

_____

_____

_____

_____

_____

_____

_____

_____

_____

_____

_____

_____

_____

_____

_____

_____

_____

_____

_____

_____

This page intentionally left blank.

PRACTICE TEST ANSWERS

PART I

1. T
2. T
3. F
4. T
5. F
6. F
7. T
8. T
9. F
10. T
11. F
12. T
13. F
14. T
15. T

PART II

1. i
2. c
3. j
4. a
5. f
6. e
7. b
8. d
9. h
10. g

PART III

1. Responsibility
2. segmentation

3. region
4. revenue
5. sales, cost of goods sold
6. apportioned
7. fair, reasonable
8. gross profit, direct
9. departmental margin
10. identical, owner's equity
11. Home Office
12. Branch, receivable
13. both
14. centralized
15. reciprocal

PART IV

1. d
2. c
3. b
4. c
5. a
6. b
7. a
8. c
9. b
10. c

PART V

Answers will vary. Please discuss questions with your instructor.

Introduction to Manufacturing Accounting

CHAPTER SUMMARY

Cost accounting is the field of accounting that is used to determine the dollar value of goods that are manufactured.

Cost is an input into the manufacturing of a product. There are three elements of cost: (1) **raw materials** are the materials used in the manufacturing process; (2) **direct labor** is the cost of those employees who work directly on the product being manufactured; and (3) **factory overhead** includes all other manufacturing costs, among which is indirect labor.

A manufacturing firm has three inventories: (1) **raw materials inventory** is the inventory of materials not yet put into production; (2) **work-in-process inventory** is the inventory of partially completed goods; and (3) **finished goods inventory** is the inventory of completed goods that are awaiting sale.

Businesses use several different types of systems to account for the costs of manufacturing. A **general accounting for manufacturing** system gathers costs throughout the year and then transfers these costs periodically to a summary account. Other systems—**job order cost accounting**, **process cost accounting**, and **standard cost accounting**—are discussed in later chapters.

A general accounting system for manufacturing uses many accounts that are different from those used for a merchandising business. Three inventory accounts, two summary accounts, purchases accounts prefaced by the words *Raw Materials*, expense controlling accounts, and various labor cost accounts are among the distinct accounts used.

Daily entries for a manufacturing firm are similar to those for a merchandising firm (except for the entries involving raw materials, direct labor, and factory overhead); however, differences appear in the adjusting entries. Old and new finished goods inventories are adjusted by using the Income Summary account; old and new raw materials and work-in-process inventories are adjusted by using the Manufacturing Summary account.

Closing entries require that all cost accounts—Raw Materials Purchases, Direct Labor, and Factory Overhead Control—be closed to the Manufacturing Summary account. Cost reduction accounts, such as Raw Materials Purchases Returns and Allowances and Raw Materials Purchases Discounts, are also closed to the Manufacturing Summary account. The balance of the Manufacturing Summary account, an amount that shows the **cost of goods manufactured**, is then closed to the Income Summary account. Other revenue and expense accounts are also closed in the usual manner to the Income Summary account.

In a general accounting system, the major manufacturing statement is the **statement of cost of goods manufactured**. This statement presents a picture of the contents of the Manufacturing Summary account. An income statement for a manufacturer replaces the net purchases of a merchandising business with the cost of goods manufactured. A balance sheet for a manufacturer is different from a balance sheet for a merchandising business in that it has three inventories listed.

This page intentionally left blank.

PRACTICE TEST

PART I TRUE/FALSE

Please circle the correct answer.

T   F   1.   Cost accounting is concerned with identifying and recording all of the costs of a product as it is manufactured.

T   F   2.   There are three elements of cost of a manufactured product.

T   F   3.   Direct labor includes the wages of the janitor who cleans the factory.

T   F   4.   A manufacturing business has three inventories.

T   F   5.   Control accounts are used by manufacturing businesses in order to maintain good internal control.

T   F   6.   A purchase of raw materials is debited to the Work-in-Process Inventory account.

T   F   7.   Indirect factory labor is debited to the Work-in-Process Inventory account.

T   F   8.   The six manufacturing accounts summarize all of the costs of the finished product.

T   F   9.   The work-in-process and raw materials inventories are adjusted at the end of the period with entries identical to those made by merchandising companies.

T   F   10.   The account used to summarize the manufacturing costs is Income Summary.

T   F   11.   After all manufacturing accounts are closed and the manufacturing inventories are adjusted, the balance in Manufacturing Summary will be the cost of goods manufactured during the period.

T   F   12.   Manufacturing Summary is closed to Income Summary.

T   F   13.   The manufacturing costs for the period are summarized on the income statement.

T   F   14.   The calculations on the statement of cost of goods manufactured for cost of raw materials used are very like those on the income statement for cost of goods sold.

T   F   15.   The total on the statement of cost of goods manufactured is transferred to the income statement in the place where net purchases are reported for a merchandising firm.

PART II MATCHING

Please match each of the following terms with its definition.

a. cost
b. cost accounting
c. cost of goods manufactured
d. direct labor
e. factory overhead

f. finished goods inventory
g. raw materials
h. raw materials inventory
i. statement of cost of goods manufactured
j. work-in-process inventory

_____ 1. The inventory of materials that have not yet been put into production.

_____ 2. The cost of employees who work directly on the product being manufactured.

_____ 3. An input into the manufacturing of a product.

_____ 4. The inventory of completed goods that are ready for sale.

_____ 5. The sum of the three elements of cost adjusted for manufacturing inventories.

_____ 6. The statement that summarizes the manufacturing costs for the period.

_____ 7. The field of accounting used to determine the dollar value of goods that are manufactured.

_____ 8. Materials used in the manufacturing process.

_____ 9. All manufacturing costs that are not raw materials or direct labor costs.

_____ 10. The inventory of partially completed goods.

PART III FILL IN THE BLANKS

Please complete each sentence with the correct word or words.

1. Cost accounting is concerned with valuing goods that are _____.

2. In accounting for manufacturing costs, the _____ elements of cost must be added to determine the total costs for the period.

3. The three elements of manufacturing cost are _____, _____, and _____.

4. In a manufacturing business, _____ are placed in production, _____ and factory overhead are added, and finished goods emerge at the end of the process.

5. A cost accounting system in which costs are collected and assigned to specific batches of work is called _____ cost accounting.

6. A system in which costs are gathered and assigned to each stage or department in the manufacturing process is called _____ cost accounting.

7. Because there are so many accounts in a manufacturing business, the accounting system uses several _____ accounts and _____ ledgers.

8. When raw materials are purchased, the _____ account is debited.

9. Indirect factory labor is debited to the _____ Control account.

10. When factory expenses are paid, the debit is to _____.

11. In a business that produces goods, transactions that do not involve _____ costs are handled the same way as similar transactions for a merchandising business.

12. There are _____ manufacturing accounts.

13. The manufacturing costs for the period are summarized on the statement of _____.

14. Manufacturing accounts are closed to the _____ account.

15. Costs of goods manufactured is shown on the income statement in the place where _____ is shown for a merchandising company.

PART IV MULTIPLE CHOICE

Please circle the correct answer.

1. Which of the following is an element of manufacturing cost?
   a. selling expense
   b. direct labor
   c. interest expense
   d. office salaries

2. Goods in the factory that have been started but are not yet completed are part of the
   a. cost of goods sold.
   b. raw materials inventory.
   c. work-in-process inventory.
   d. finished goods inventory.

3. The wages of a machine operator who drills holes for screws in the product would be debited to
   a. Work-in-Process Inventory.
   b. Factory Overhead Control.
   c. Wages Payable.
   d. Direct Labor.

4. The wages of the security guard at the factory would be debited to
   a. Work-in-Process Inventory.
   b. Factory Overhead Control.
   c. Wages Payable.
   d. Direct Labor.

5. A system of accounting in which costs are gathered throughout the year and transferred periodically to a summary account is called
   a. general accounting for manufacturing.
   b. job order cost accounting.
   c. process cost accounting.
   d. standard cost accounting.

6. Most manufacturing businesses use several control accounts and subsidiary ledgers
   a. because there are so many accounts in a manufacturing business.
   b. to reduce the number of general ledger accounts needed and keep the general ledger from becoming unwieldy.
   c. that are handled the same way as the control accounts and subsidiary ledgers for payables and receivables.
   d. all of the above.

7. When recording manufacturing costs it is sometimes helpful to ask, "Is it raw materials?" and "Is it direct labor?" If it is not, then it is
   a. factory overhead.
   b. general expense.
   c. operating expense.
   d. other expense.

8. When the beginning balance of the finished goods inventory is closed, the debit is to
   a. Manufacturing Summary.
   b. Income Summary.
   c. Retained Earnings.
   d. Finished Goods Inventory.

9. When the ending balances of the raw materials and work-in-process inventories are recorded, the credit is to
   a. Manufacturing Summary.
   b. Income Summary.
   c. Retained Earnings.
   d. Finished Goods Inventory.

10. The financial statement that is prepared only by a manufacturing business
    a. is the statement of cost of goods manufactured.
    b. summarizes manufacturing costs for the period.
    c. is used to compute the cost of goods manufactured, which is needed for the income statement.
    d. all of the above.

PART V WRITING/SHORT ANSWER

1. **Reflect** Make a list, in words or simple phrases, of the most important and meaningful points in this chapter.

2. **Question** Think about the most confusing points or the material you do not understand in this chapter. Write down two or three questions that remain unanswered.

3. **Connect** Explain, in one or two sentences, the connection between the main points of this chapter and the major goals of the entire course.

4. **Summarize** Review this chapter's Joining the Pieces visual summary and explain the concept(s) illustrated in a few sentences.

WORKING PAPERS

SKILLS REVIEW

EXERCISE 25-1

General Journal

	Date	Account Title	P.R.	Debit	Credit	
1						1
2						2
3						3
4						4
5						5
6						6
7						7
8						8
9						9
10						10
11						11
12						12
13						13
14						14
15						15
16						16
17						17
18						18
19						19
20						20
21						21
22						22
23						23
24						24
25						25
26						26
27						27
28						28
29						29
30						30
31						31
32						32

EXERCISE 25-2

General Journal

	Date		Account Title	P.R.	Debit	Credit	
1							1
2							2
3							3
4							4
5							5
6							6
7							7
8							8
9							9
10							10
11							11
12							12
13							13
14							14
15							15
16							16
17							17
18							18
19							19
20							20
21							21
22							22
23							23
24							24
25							25
26							26
27							27
28							28
29							29
30							30
31							31
32							32

EXERCISE 25-3

General Journal

	Date		Account Title	P.R.	Debit	Credit	
1							1
2							2
3							3
4							4
5							5
6							6
7							7
8							8
9							9
10							10
11							11
12							12
13							13
14							14
15							15
16							16
17							17
18							18
19							19
20							20
21							21
22							22
23							23
24							24
25							25
26							26
27							27
28							28
29							29
30							30
31							31
32							32

EXERCISE 25-4

EXERCISE 25-5

EXERCISE 25-6

CASE PROBLEMS

PROBLEM 25-1A OR 25-1B

General Journal

Page 1

	Date		Account Title	P.R.	Debit	Credit	
1							1
2							2
3							3
4							4
5							5
6							6
7							7
8							8
9							9
10							10
11							11
12							12
13							13
14							14
15							15
16							16
17							17
18							18
19							19
20							20
21							21
22							22
23							23
24							24
25							25
26							26
27							27
28							28
29							29
30							30
31							31
32							32

This page intentionally left blank.

This page intentionally left blank.

PROBLEM 25-2A OR 25-2B

(Left side)

Account Title	Trial Balance		Adjustments	
	Dr.	Cr.	Dr.	Cr.

(Right side)

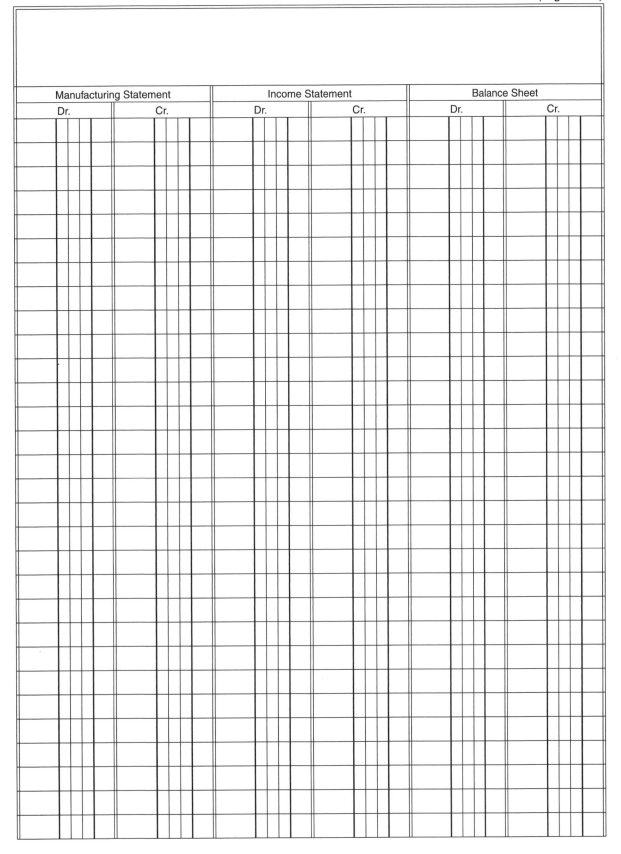

	Manufacturing Statement		Income Statement		Balance Sheet	
	Dr.	Cr.	Dr.	Cr.	Dr.	Cr.

This page intentionally left blank.

PROBLEM 25-3A OR 25-3B

General Journal

	Date	Account Title	P.R.	Debit	Credit	
1						1
2						2
3						3
4						4
5						5
6						6
7						7
8						8
9						9
10						10
11						11
12						12
13						13
14						14
15						15
16						16
17						17
18						18
19						19
20						20
21						21
22						22
23						23
24						24
25						25
26						26
27						27
28						28
29						29
30						30
31						31
32						32

ACCOUNT Income Summary   ACCOUNT NO. 331

DATE	ITEM	P.R.	DEBIT	CREDIT	BALANCE	
					DEBIT	CREDIT

ACCOUNT Manufacturing Summary   ACCOUNT NO. 332

DATE	ITEM	P.R.	DEBIT	CREDIT	BALANCE	
					DEBIT	CREDIT

PROBLEM 25-4A OR 25-4B

This page intentionally left blank.

This page intentionally left blank.

PROBLEM 25-6A OR 25-6B

1.

General Journal

	Date	Account Title	P.R.	Debit	Credit	
1						1
2						2
3						3
4						4
5						5
6						6
7						7
8						8
9						9
10						10
11						11
12						12
13						13
14						14
15						15
16						16
17						17
18						18
19						19
20						20
21						21
22						22
23						23
24						24
25						25
26						26
27						27
28						28
29						29
30						30
31						31
32						32

2., 3.   **General Journal**   Page 2

	Date		Account Title	P.R.	Debit	Credit	
1			Adjusting Entries				1
2							2
3							3
4							4
5							5
6							6
7							7
8							8
9							9
10							10
11							11
12							12
13			Closing Entries				13
14							14
15							15
16							16
17							17
18							18
19							19
20							20
21							21
22							22
23							23
24							24
25							25
26							26
27							27
28							28
29							29
30							30
31							31
32							32

4.

5.

CHALLENGE PROBLEMS

PROBLEM SOLVING

	Work-in-Pro. Beg.	Raw Mat. Beg.	Raw. Mat. Purch.	Raw. Mat. Avail.	Raw. Mat. End.	Cost Raw Mat. Used
(a)						
(b)						
(c)						
(d)						

	Labor and Overhead	Total Mfg. Cost	Total Goods in Production	Work-in-Pro. End.	Cost of Goods Mfd.
(a)					
(b)					
(c)					
(d)					

This page intentionally left blank.

COMMUNICATIONS

ETHICS

This page intentionally left blank.

PRACTICE TEST ANSWERS

PART I

1. T
2. T
3. F
4. T
5. F
6. F
7. F
8. T
9. F
10. F
11. T
12. T
13. F
14. T
15. T

PART II

1. h
2. d
3. a
4. f
5. c
6. i
7. b
8. g
9. e
10. j

PART III

1. manufactured
2. three
3. raw materials, direct labor, factory overhead

4. raw materials, direct labor
5. job order
6. process
7. control, subsidiary
8. Raw Materials Purchases
9. Factory Overhead
10. Factory Overhead Control
11. manufacturing
12. six
13. cost of goods manufactured
14. Manufacturing Summary
15. net purchases

PART IV

1. b
2. c
3. d
4. b
5. a
6. d
7. a
8. b
9. a
10. d

PART V

Answers will vary. Please discuss questions with your instructor.

Job Order and Process Cost Accounting

CHAPTER SUMMARY

Job order cost accounting, one of the "true" cost accounting systems, is a way of keeping track of costs by jobs or batches of work. All three elements of cost are accumulated for each job, so at the conclusion of the job, total costs and per unit costs for that job can be determined.

The flow of costs in a job order system is from each element into work-in-process into finished goods into cost of goods sold.

Accounting for raw materials in a job order system involves entries and subsidiary records for purchases, returns, and the issuance of materials to production. A job order system uses a *perpetual inventory system*, a running record of what is on hand. Thus, all additions to the amount of raw materials are debited to a Raw Materials Inventory account, while all subtractions are credited to that account. **Materials ledger records** serve as a subsidiary ledger for the Raw Materials Inventory account.

While no distinction is made as to the type of material in purchasing and returning materials, a clear distinction is made when materials are issued to production. **Direct materials**, which are identifiable components of the finished product, are debited to the Work-in-Process Inventory account. **Indirect materials**, such as factory supplies, are debited to the Factory Overhead Control account. When materials are issued to production, the materials ledger records are updated. The total of all the balances in these records should equal the balance of the Raw Materials Inventory account.

Labor costs are recorded in a Payroll account when they are incurred. The costs that make up the Payroll account balance are then transferred to the appropriate accounts. The Work-in-Process Inventory account is debited for **direct labor** (the cost of employees who worked directly on the finished product), and the Factory Overhead Control account is debited for **indirect labor** (the cost of factory employees who did not work directly on the finished product). Other amounts are charged to the Selling and General Expense Control accounts.

Factory overhead—the cost of running a factory—is accumulated as it is paid or through adjusting entries. It is charged to production at a predetermined rate, usually a percent of the direct labor cost.

The Work-in-Process Inventory account contains all three cost elements. This account is supported by **individual job sheets**, subsidiary records that show the costs accumulated for each job. Goods completed are transferred to the Finished Goods Inventory account, which is supported by **finished goods inventory records**. When goods are sold, their costs are transferred to the Cost of Goods Sold account.

At the end of each accounting period, the balance of the Factory Overhead Control account is transferred to the Cost of Goods Sold account. If too little overhead has been charged to production, overhead is **underapplied**. The following entry is then made:

        Cost of Goods Sold
            Factory Overhead Control

If too much overhead has been charged to production, the overhead is **overapplied**. The following entry is then made:

        Factory Overhead Control
            Cost of Goods Sold

The final step in the job order cost system is to record the sales price of goods in the usual way.

Process cost accounting is a way of keeping track of costs by production department. The flow of costs in a process system is from the three elements of cost into the first production department and then into the second department and so forth. Direct labor and factory overhead are always added in all departments, while materials are sometimes not added after the first department. Departmental work-in-process costs flow into finished goods and then into cost of goods sold.

The entries made for purchases and returns of raw materials and for incurring labor and overhead costs are identical to those in job order cost accounting. Entries to issue materials to production, charge labor costs, and estimate overhead costs as a percent of direct labor costs are also similar to those made in a job order system, except that a separate work-in-process account is used for each department.

To transfer goods from department to department, the following entry is made:

        Work-in-Process Inventory—Dept. B
            Work-in-Process Inventory—Dept. A

The amount recorded in this entry is calculated by multiplying the number of units transferred by the cost per unit. To determine the cost per unit, **equivalent units**—the work actually done—must be calculated. If 1,200 units were put into production, 900 are finished, and the remaining 300 are 1/3 finished, equivalent units are $900 + 1/3(300) = 1,000$ units.

All of the units and costs transferred into and out of a production department are recorded in a **cost of production report**. Both units and costs are explained in order to account for the processing in that department.

The final entries in a process cost accounting system are identical to those in a job order cost accounting system.

PRACTICE TEST

PART I TRUE/FALSE

Please circle the correct answer.

T F 1. A true cost accounting system accumulates the costs of production only when production is complete.

T F 2. Job order cost accounting keeps track of production costs by job or batch of units being produced.

T F 3. In the perpetual inventory method, all purchases are debited to an inventory account.

T F 4. Perpetual inventory records for the various types of raw materials used by a firm are maintained in the general ledger.

T F 5. The sum of all balances in the factory overhead subsidiary ledger should equal the balance in the Factory Overhead Control account.

T F 6. Factory overhead is usually charged to production by using a predetermined rate.

T F 7. Debits to the Work-in-Process Inventory account equal the total of the costs charged to production.

T F 8. Individual job cost sheets are used to keep a record of finished goods.

T F 9. Subsidiary ledger records for finished goods look very like those for raw materials.

T F 10. When finished units are sold, the cost of the units is debited to Finished Goods Inventory and credited to Cost of Goods Sold.

T F 11. Overapplied factory overhead occurs when more overhead is charged to production than was incurred during the period.

T F 12. In process cost accounting, costs are accumulated by job.

T F 13. Perpetual inventories are maintained when a process cost accounting system is used.

T F 14. In process cost accounting, each production department in the factory must calculate its equivalent units of production.

T F 15. In a process cost system, each production department must account for every unit and every dollar charged to it.

T F 16. A cost of production report is necessary in a job order system.

T F 17. The first section of a cost of production report shows the costs that entered the department.

T F 18. Equivalent units are used to calculate the cost per unit in a process cost system.

T F 19. Department 2 receives units and costs from Department 1 and must use these to calculate the units produced and the cost per unit in Department 2.

T F 20. In a process cost system, every production department must prepare a cost of production report.

PART II MATCHING

Please match each of the following terms with its definition.

a. cost of production report
b. direct labor
c. direct materials
d. equivalent units
e. factory overhead
f. finished goods inventory records
g. indirect labor
h. indirect materials

i. individual job sheets
j. job order cost accounting
k. materials ledger records
l. overapplied overhead
m. perpetual inventory
n. process cost accounting
o. underapplied overhead

_____ 1. A way of keeping track of costs by job or by groups of items that are produced at one time.

_____ 2. A running balance of items on hand.

_____ 3. Records used in a perpetual inventory system that show the cost of items purchased as raw materials.

_____ 4. Materials that are an identifiable part of the finished product.

_____ 5. Materials that are needed in the production process but are not an identifiable part of the finished product.

_____ 6. Employees who work directly on the finished product.

_____ 7. Factory employees, such as janitors and supervisors, who do not work directly on the finished product.

_____ 8. The costs of running a factory.

_____ 9. Subsidiary records that show the costs accumulated for every job.

_____ 10. Subsidiary records that show completed goods received and sold.

_____ 11. Occurs when too little overhead is charged to production.

_____ 12. Occurs when too much overhead is charged to production.

_____ 13. A method of keeping track of costs by production department rather than by job.

_____ 14. The work actually done by a production department in a process cost system.

_____ 15. Reports all of the units and costs transferred into and out of a production department in a process cost system.

PART III FILL IN THE BLANKS

Please complete each sentence with the correct word or words.

1. A(n) _____ inventory record is maintained for raw materials in a job order or process cost accounting system because it is important to know what and how much is on hand.

2. When a purchase of materials is made, the debit is to _____.

3. Purchases of materials must also be posted to the _____.

4. When materials are issued to production, the direct materials are debited to _____ and the indirect materials are debited to _____.

5. When charging payroll to production, the cost of direct labor is _____ to Work-in-Process Inventory.

6. A(n) _____ rate is usually used to charge factory overhead to production.

7. When factory overhead is charged to production, _____ is debited and _____ is credited.

8. The costs of finished goods are transferred out of the Work-in-Process Inventory account by _____ Finished Goods Inventory and _____ Work-in-Process Inventory.

9. As finished goods are sold, the cost of the items sold is recorded by a debit to _____.

10. Any overapplied or underapplied overhead is closed to _____.

11. In a process cost accounting system, a separate Work-in-Process Inventory account must be maintained for each _____.

12. In process costing, materials, labor, and _____ are charged to each production department's Work-in-Process Inventory account.

13. _____ units represent work actually done.

14. To transfer costs from Department A to Department B, the debit is to Work-in-Process Inventory— _____.

15. On a cost of production report, each production department must account for all _____ and all _____ charged to it.

PART IV MULTIPLE CHOICE

Please circle the correct answer.

1. A true cost accounting system accumulates costs
   a. at the end of the period.
   b. as production is ongoing.
   c. when the job is complete.
   d. when the units are sold.

2. The flow of costs in a job order system is
   a. from raw materials, direct labor, and factory overhead into work-in-process.
   b. from work-in-process into finished goods.
   c. from finished goods into cost of goods sold.
   d. all of the above.

3. The balance in the Work-in-Process Inventory account at the end of the period represents
   a. the cost of work still in production.
   b. the cost of finished goods.
   c. the cost of materials and labor.
   d. none of the above.

4. An individual job sheet shows
   a. the cost of the materials and direct labor used on the job.
   b. the factory overhead applied to the job.
   c. the unit cost of the items produced for the job.
   d. all of the above.

5. An account needed for a perpetual inventory system that is not used with a periodic inventory system is
   a. Cost of Goods Sold.
   b. Finished Goods Inventory.
   c. Purchases.
   d. Raw Materials Inventory.

6. Factory overhead is overapplied when
   a. more overhead is incurred than is charged to Work-in-Process Inventory.
   b. more overhead is incurred than is budgeted.
   c. more overhead is charged to Work-in Process Inventory than is incurred.
   d. none of the above.

7. In a process cost accounting system,
   a. materials can only be placed into production in the first department.
   b. direct labor and overhead are added in each department.
   c. each department's completed products are transferred to finished goods.
   d. each job is treated as a separate department.

8. In order to calculate equivalent units, the following information is needed:
   a. actual units left in the department at the end of the period.
   b. the amount of work that has been done on the units in process.
   c. actual units completed during the period.
   d. all of the above.

9. The first schedule to appear in a cost of production report shows
   a. costs charged to the department.
   b. number of units charged to the department.
   c. unit costs.
   d. distribution of costs.

10. Which of the following is not shown on a cost of production report?
    a. cost of goods sold
    b. unit costs of items produced
    c. equivalent units
    d. the three elements of manufacturing cost

PART V WRITING/SHORT ANSWER

1. **Reflect** Make a list, in words or simple phrases, of the most important and meaningful points in this chapter.

2. **Question** Think about the most confusing points or the material you do not understand in this chapter. Write down two or three questions that remain unanswered.

3. **Connect** Explain, in one or two sentences, the connection between the main points of this chapter and the major goals of the entire course.

4. **Summarize** Review this chapter's Joining the Pieces visual summary and explain the concept(s) illustrated in a few sentences.

WORKING PAPERS

SKILLS REVIEW

EXERCISE 26-1

1.

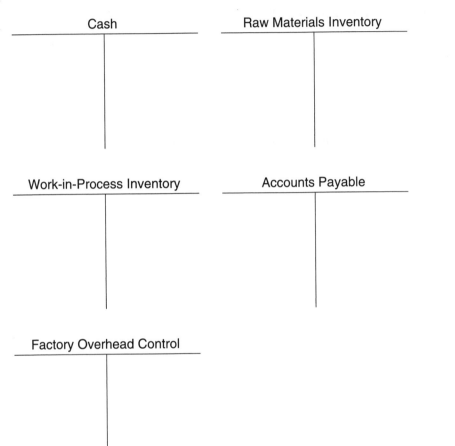

Cash

Raw Materials Inventory

Work-in-Process Inventory

Accounts Payable

Factory Overhead Control

2. The balance of the Raw Materials Inventory account is _____ .

EXERCISE 26-2

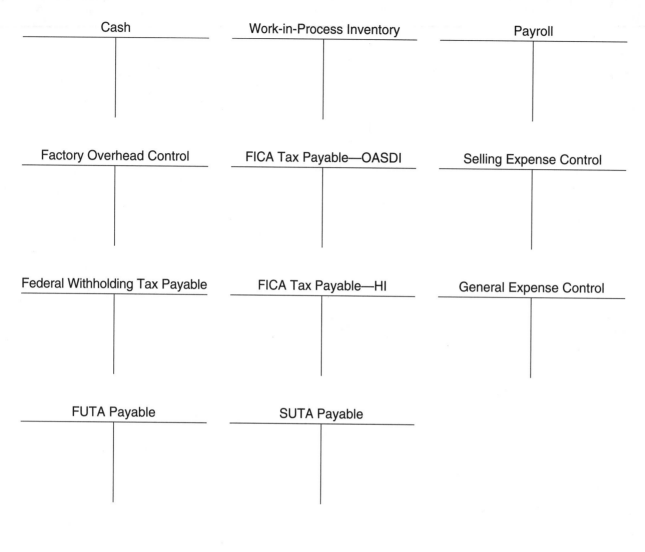

| Cash | | Work-in-Process Inventory | | Payroll |
| | | |

| Factory Overhead Control | | FICA Tax Payable—OASDI | | Selling Expense Control |

| Federal Withholding Tax Payable | | FICA Tax Payable—HI | | General Expense Control |

| FUTA Payable | | SUTA Payable |

EXERCISE 26-3

	Date	Account Title	P.R.	Debit	Credit	
1						1
2						2
3						3
4						4
5						5
6						6
7						7
8						8
9						9
10						10
11						11
12						12
13						13
14						14
15						15
16						16
17						17

EXERCISE 26-4

General Journal

	Date		Account Title	P.R.	Debit	Credit	
1							1
2							2
3							3
4							4
5							5
6							6
7							7
8							8
9							9
10							10
11							11
12							12
13							13
14							14
15							15
16							16
17							17
18							18
19							19
20							20
21							21
22							22
23							23
24							24
25							25
26							26
27							27
28							28
29							29
30							30
31							31
32							32

EXERCISE 26-5

General Journal   Page 1

	Date	Account Title	P.R.	Debit	Credit	
1						1
2						2
3						3
4						4
5						5
6						6
7						7
8						8
9						9
10						10
11						11
12						12
13						13
14						14
15						15
16						16
17						17
18						18

EXERCISE 26-6

Equivalent Units

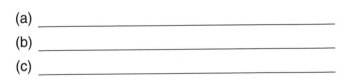

(a) _____

(b) _____

(c) _____

EXERCISE 26-7

	Date		Account Title	P.R.	Debit	Credit	
1							1
2							2
3							3
4							4
5							5
6							6
7							7
8							8
9							9
10							10
11							11
12							12
13							13
14							14
15							15
16							16
17							17
18							18
19							19
20							20
21							21
22							22
23							23
24							24
25							25
26							26
27							27
28							28
29							29
30							30
31							31
32							32

CASE PROBLEMS

PROBLEM 26-1A OR 26-1B

1., 3.

ACCOUNT Raw Materials Inventory   ACCOUNT NO. 108

DATE	ITEM	P.R.	DEBIT	CREDIT	BALANCE DEBIT	BALANCE CREDIT

Item ____ Material A ____

DATE	RECEIVED	ISSUED	BALANCE

Item ____ Material B ____

DATE	RECEIVED	ISSUED	BALANCE

4. _____

2.   **General Journal**   Page 1

	Date		Account Title	P.R.	Debit	Credit	
1							1
2							2
3							3
4							4
5							5
6							6
7							7
8							8
9							9
10							10
11							11
12							12
13							13
14							14

PROBLEM SOLVING

1.

(a) Cost of the units transferred to Department B = _____

(b) Value of the work-in-process inventory at the end of January = _____

PROBLEM SOLVING (continued)

2.

(a) Cost of the units transferred to Department B, assuming FIFO = _____

(b) Value of the work-in-process inventory at the end of February = _____

COMMUNICATIONS

_____

_____

_____

_____

_____

_____

_____

_____

_____

_____

_____

_____

_____

_____

_____

_____

_____

_____

ETHICS

_____

_____

_____

_____

_____

_____

_____

_____

_____

_____

_____

_____

_____

_____

_____

_____

_____

_____

This page intentionally left blank.

PRACTICE TEST ANSWERS

PART I

1. F
2. T
3. T
4. F
5. T
6. T
7. T
8. F
9. T
10. F
11. T
12. F
13. T
14. T
15. T
16. F
17. F
18. T
19. T
20. T

PART II

1. j
2. m
3. k
4. c
5. h
6. b
7. g
8. e
9. i
10. f
11. o
12. l
13. n
14. d
15. a

PART III

1. perpetual
2. Raw Materials Inventory
3. materials ledger records
4. Work-in-Process Inventory, Factory Overhead Control
5. debited
6. predetermined
7. Work-in-Process Inventory, Factory Overhead Control
8. debiting, crediting
9. Cost of Goods Sold
10. Cost of Goods Sold
11. production department
12. overhead
13. Equivalent
14. Department B
15. units, costs

PART IV

1. b
2. d
3. a
4. d
5. a
6. c
7. b
8. d
9. b
10. a

PART V

Answers will vary. Please discuss questions with your instructor.

WORKING PAPERS

General Journal

	Date	Account Title	P.R.	Debit	Credit	
1						1
2						2
3						3
4						4
5						5
6						6
7						7
8						8
9						9
10						10
11						11
12						12
13						13
14						14
15						15
16						16
17						17
18						18
19						19
20						20
21						21
22						22
23						23
24						24
25						25
26						26
27						27
28						28
29						29
30						30
31						31
32						32

	Date		Account Title	P.R.	Debit	Credit	
1							1
2							2
3							3
4							4
5							5
6							6
7							7
8							8
9							9
10							10
11							11
12							12
13							13
14							14
15							15
16							16
17							17
18							18
19							19
20							20
21							21
22							22
23							23
24							24
25							25
26							26
27							27
28							28
29							29
30							30
31							31
32							32

	Date	Account Title	P.R.	Debit	Credit	
1						1
2						2
3						3
4						4
5						5
6						6
7						7
8						8
9						9
10						10
11						11
12						12
13						13
14						14
15						15
16						16
17						17
18						18
19						19
20						20
21						21
22						22
23						23
24						24
25						25
26						26
27						27
28						28
29						29
30						30
31						31
32						32

General Ledger

ACCOUNT Raw Materials Inventory   ACCOUNT NO. 108

DATE	ITEM	P.R.	DEBIT	CREDIT	BALANCE DEBIT	BALANCE CREDIT

ACCOUNT Work-in-Process Inventory   ACCOUNT NO. 109

DATE	ITEM	P.R.	DEBIT	CREDIT	BALANCE DEBIT	BALANCE CREDIT

ACCOUNT Finished Goods Inventory   ACCOUNT NO. 110

DATE	ITEM	P.R.	DEBIT	CREDIT	BALANCE DEBIT	BALANCE CREDIT

ACCOUNT Cost of Goods Sold   ACCOUNT NO. 440

DATE	ITEM	P.R.	DEBIT	CREDIT	BALANCE DEBIT	BALANCE CREDIT

ACCOUNT Factory Overhead Control   ACCOUNT NO. 470

DATE	ITEM	P.R.	DEBIT	CREDIT	BALANCE DEBIT	BALANCE CREDIT

MATERIALS LEDGER RECORD—ROSINE

Received			Issued			Balance			
Rec. Report Number	Quantity	Amount	Mat. Req. Number	Quantity	Amount	Date	Quantity	Amount	Unit Cost

MATERIALS LEDGER RECORD—EMOLINE

Received			Issued			Balance			
Rec. Report Number	Quantity	Amount	Mat. Req. Number	Quantity	Amount	Date	Quantity	Amount	Unit Cost

MATERIALS LEDGER RECORD—FACTORY SUPPLIES

Received			Issued			Balance			
Rec. Report Number	Quantity	Amount	Mat. Req. Number	Quantity	Amount	Date	Quantity	Amount	Unit Cost

FINISHED GOODS INVENTORY RECORD—CANLETS

Manufactured			Shipped			Balance		Cost	
Job Order No.	Quantity	Total Cost	Ship. Order No.	Quantity	Total Cost	Date	Quantity	Total	Unit

Individual Job Sheets

Job No. _____   Item _____
Date Begun _____   Date Finished _____

DATE		DIRECT MATERIALS	DIRECT LABOR	FACTORY OVERHEAD
Totals				

Total Cost _____   Unit Cost _____

Job No. _____   Item _____
Date Begun _____   Date Finished _____

DATE		DIRECT MATERIALS	DIRECT LABOR	FACTORY OVERHEAD
Totals				

Total Cost _____   Unit Cost _____

Job No. _____   Item _____
Date Begun _____   Date Finished _____

DATE		DIRECT MATERIALS	DIRECT LABOR	FACTORY OVERHEAD
Totals				

Total Cost _____   Unit Cost _____

27 Budgeting and Standard Cost Accounting

CHAPTER SUMMARY

A **budget** is a formal statement, in financial terms, of management's plans for the future. Budgets are prepared for all parts of operations and for all types of assets. The keys to successful budgeting are (1) to make accurate forecasts of the future and (2) to compare actual results with those that were forecasted. By doing this, a business can assign responsibility for costs and revenue and, hopefully, increase net income.

There are various types of budgets, depending on the needs of the individual business. Service businesses often prepare budgets for revenue, operating expenses, and cash. Merchandising businesses prepare the same budgets as well as budgets for sales, purchases, and cost of goods sold. A manufacturer likewise prepares these budgets and in addition prepares budgets for materials, labor, factory overhead, and cost of goods manufactured. This chapter focuses on budgets needed by a manufacturer.

Most businesses budget for the **fiscal year**. To meet its individual needs, however, a firm can choose to budget for longer periods of time or shorter periods of time. A common practice is to budget for a year in advance but then break that year's budget into budgets for four quarters of three months each. At the end of each quarter, actual results are compared with planned results. Action can then be taken if differences exist between budgeted amounts and actual amounts.

A common way for a manufacturer to budget is to prepare income statement budgets and balance sheet budgets. Income statement budgets include a **sales budget**, a **production budget**, a **direct materials purchases budget**, a **direct labor cost budget**, a **factory overhead budget**, a **cost of goods manufactured budget**, a **cost of goods sold budget**, and an **operating expenses budget**. All of these individual budgets then come together to form the **budgeted income statement**, the end result of which is a planned net income figure for the period.

When preparing balance sheet budgets, it is possible to forecast each item of assets, liabilities, and owner's equity. This chapter focuses on two budgets as examples of balance sheet budgets: the **cash budget** and the **capital expenditures budget**. The cash budget is a budget that estimates the cash to be received and spent during a period of time. The cash budget is used for short-term planning. The capital expenditures budget is used for long-term planning. This budget focuses on when plant assets will need to be replaced so that expenditures for these assets can be planned.

Estimates of cash and capital expenditures are combined with estimates of other assets, liabilities, and owner's equity to form the **budgeted balance sheet**. The budgeted balance sheet estimates each element of financial condition at a specified future time.

Budgets are sometimes prepared on the assumption that a fixed quantity of units will be produced. However, some firms prepare a **flexible budget** in order to provide in advance for possible changes in the level of production. A flexible budget is, in reality, a series of budgets for different levels of production activity.

When a flexible budget is prepared, costs must be classified as variable and fixed. A **variable cost** is one that varies (in total) as production varies, such as direct materials and direct labor. A **fixed cost** is one that remains the same (in total) as production levels change. An example of a fixed cost is factory rent; the rent remains the same whether the company is producing 1,000 units or 10,000 units.

Some manufacturers use a **standard cost accounting** system. In this system, which is based on budgets, costs are assigned to manufactured products in advance. These budgeted costs (or standard costs) are then adjusted to the actual costs at the end of the accounting period. Any difference in actual costs from standard costs is termed a **variance**. If actual costs exceed budgeted costs, there is an **unfavorable variance**. If actual costs are less than budgeted costs, there is a **favorable variance**.

Variances are broken down into the elements of cost. Thus, there is a **direct materials variance**, a **direct labor variance**, and a **factory overhead variance**. The direct materials variance is subdivided into two types: the **direct materials price variance** and the **direct materials quantity variance**. The direct labor variance is subdivided into two types: the **direct labor rate variance** and the **direct labor time variance** (also called the **labor efficiency variance**). All variances, whether favorable or unfavorable, should be analyzed to determine why they occurred.

PRACTICE TEST

PART I TRUE/FALSE

Please circle the correct answer.

T   F   1. A budget is a formal written statement of management's financial plans for the future.

T   F   2. It is a common practice to budget revenues as well as costs.

T   F   3. Only private, profit-making companies need to budget.

T   F   4. The time period for which budgets are prepared varies with the person or firm preparing the budget.

T   F   5. Budgets for more than a year are never made because of the difficulty of forecasting that far in advance.

T   F   6. An income statement budget is actually the end result of a number of individual budgets of income statement data.

T   F   7. A sales budget should only be prepared by a merchandising business.

T   F   8. The direct materials purchases budget is concerned *only* with the number of units of raw materials that will be needed to meet a firm's production needs.

T   F   9. The cost of goods manufactured budget is always the first budget prepared by a manufacturing firm.

T   F   10. There is no need to prepare an operating expenses budget since most expenses are beyond the control of management.

T   F   11. The cash budget is planned on a month-by-month basis over a fiscal year.

T   F   12. The capital expenditures budget is used for long-term planning.

T   F   13. A flexible budget is actually a series of budgets for different levels of production.

T   F   14. Costs that vary in total but remain the same per unit are called variable costs.

T   F   15. Costs that are fixed in total but vary per unit are called fixed costs.

T   F   16. A variance results when actual costs for a period differ from standard costs for the same period.

T   F   17. If actual costs exceed standard costs, there is an unfavorable variance.

T   F   18. If actual costs are less than standard costs, there is a favorable variance.

T   F   19. The direct materials variance can be broken down into a quantity variance and a price variance.

T   F   20. The direct labor time variance explains the amount of variance between the number of direct labor hours used and the budgeted direct labor hours.

PART II MATCHING

Please match each of the following terms with its definition.

a. balance sheet budgets   f. fixed costs
b. budget   g. flexible budget
c. budget period   h. income statement budgets
d. cash budget   i. variable costs
e. capital expenditures budget   j. variance

_____ 1. The period of time covered by a budget.

_____ 2. The difference between actual costs and standard costs.

_____ 3. A series of budgets leading to budgeted assets, liabilities, and owner's equity.

_____ 4. A statement, in financial terms, of management's plans for the future.

_____ 5. Costs that vary in total as production levels change but remain fixed per unit.

_____ 6. A budget showing expected month-by-month cash activity during an upcoming fiscal year.

_____ 7. Costs that remain the same in total as production levels change but vary per unit.

_____ 8. A series of budgets leading to budgeted revenues, expenses, and net income.

_____ 9. A series of budgets for different levels of production activity.

_____ 10. A long-term budget that focuses on when plant assets will need to be replaced.

PART III FILL IN THE BLANKS

Please complete each sentence with the correct word or words.

1. In accounting, planning is expressed by preparing a(n) _____.

2. An accounting system in which manufacturing costs are budgeted and later compared with actual costs is the _____ cost accounting system.

3. A(n) _____ budget is an estimate of the total dollar volume of sales revenue for the upcoming fiscal period.

4. A(n) _____ budget estimates the number of units to be produced in the upcoming fiscal period.

5. The _____ budget is an estimate of the cash to be received and to be spent over a period of time.

6. The _____ budget is used for long-term planning of plant asset needs.

7. The budgeted _____ estimates each element of financial condition at a specified future time.

8. A(n) _____ budget is really a series of budgets for different levels of production activity.

9. A(n) _____ cost is one that varies in total as production levels change but remains constant per unit.

10. A(n) _____ cost is one that remains fixed in total as production levels change but varies per unit.

11. The difference between an actual cost and a budgeted cost is termed a(n) _____.

12. If actual costs are greater than standard costs, there is a(n) _____ variance.

13. The direct materials _____ variance results from a difference between the actual quantity used and the budgeted quantity.

14. The direct labor _____ variance explains the amount of variance between the number of direct labor hours used and the budgeted direct labor hours.

15. The direct labor _____ variance explains the amount of variance between the actual cost per hour of direct labor and the budgeted cost per hour.

PART IV MULTIPLE CHOICE

Please circle the correct answer.

1. Budgeting is needed by
   a. only profit-making businesses.
   b. all organizations except for governmental units.
   c. all organizations.
   d. all organizations and individuals.

2. Business firms usually budget
   a. for the fiscal year.
   b. only on a monthly basis.
   c. only for a year or more.
   d. daily.

3. A sales budget is
   a. an estimate of the total dollar volume of sales for the upcoming fiscal year.
   b. an estimate consisting only of the number of units to be sold in the upcoming fiscal year.
   c. a series of budgets that show the estimated net income for the upcoming fiscal year.
   d. prepared only by a merchandising firm.

4. An operating expenses budget
   a. considers all production costs for the upcoming fiscal period.
   b. considers only factory overhead items.
   c. involves the estimated selling and general expenses for the upcoming fiscal period.
   d. is not needed in a manufacturing firm because all expenses are production related.

5. The cash budget is
   a. a budget concerning a firm's long-term cash needs.
   b. needed only by businesses that are suffering from cash-flow problems.
   c. a month-by-month estimate of the cash to be received and spent during the upcoming fiscal year.
   d. needed only by large firms.

6. The capital expenditures budget is
   a. used for long-term planning of the acquisition of plant assets.
   b. used to project stockholders' equity for the upcoming fiscal period.
   c. used to estimate the cash needed over the next five years.
   d. used only by manufacturing firms that have a large investment in long-term assets.

7. A flexible budget is
   a. a complete list of a firm's budgets.
   b. one that changes from period to period.
   c. a series of budgets for different levels of production activity.
   d. used only when production levels are expected to increase.

8. Variable costs are costs that
   a. vary only if production levels decrease.
   b. vary in total as production levels change.
   c. vary only if production levels increase.
   d. stay the same in total, but vary per unit.

9. The difference between an actual and a budgeted cost is termed
   a. a variable cost.
   b. a fixed cost.
   c. a standard cost.
   d. a variance.

10. The direct materials price variance
    a. explains why the amount of direct materials used differs from the standard quantity.
    b. explains why the unit cost of materials differs from the standard cost.
    c. explains the difference between the price paid for direct materials and the standard price.
    d. is calculated only if the price paid for materials is greater than the budgeted price.

PART V WRITING/SHORT ANSWER

1. **Reflect** Make a list, in words or simple phrases, of the most important and meaningful points in this chapter.

2. **Question** Think about the most confusing points or the material you do not understand in this chapter. Write down two or three questions that remain unanswered.

3. **Connect** Explain, in one or two sentences, the connection between the main points of this chapter and the major goals of the entire course.

4. **Summarize** Review this chapter's Joining the Pieces visual summary and explain the concept(s) illustrated in a few sentences.

WORKING PAPERS

SKILLS REVIEW

EXERCISE 27-1

Westminster Corporation Sales Budget 20X1	Marfax				Colfax				Total			

Westminster Corporation Production Budget 20X1	Marfax				Colfax			

Foxhurst Corporation

Direct Materials Purchases Budget

20X1

	Magnum				

Foxhurst Corporation

Direct Labor Cost Budget

20X1

Foxhurst Corporation

Factory Overhead Budget

20X1

Foxhurst Corporation

Cost of Goods Manufactured Budget

20X1

EXERCISE 27-3

Spencer Corporation Income Statement For Year Ending December 31, 20X1													

Allen Corporation															
Cash Budget															
January, 20X1															

EXERCISE 27-5

Stanhope Corporation Flexible Budget 20X1		
	UNITS	
	1,000	2,000

EXERCISE 27-6

(a) _____

_____

_____

_____

_____

(b) _____

_____

_____

_____

_____

(c) _____

_____

_____

_____

_____

EXERCISE 27-7

(a) _____

_____

_____

_____

_____

(b) _____

_____

_____

_____

_____

(c) _____

_____

_____

_____

_____

General Journal

	Date	Account Title	P.R.	Debit	Credit	
1						1
2						2
3						3
4						4
5						5
6						6
7						7
8						8
9						9
10						10
11						11
12						12
13						13
14						14
15						15
16						16
17						17
18						18
19						19
20						20
21						21
22						22
23						23
24						24
25						25
26						26
27						27
28						28
29						29
30						30
31						31
32						32

This page intentionally left blank.

CHALLENGE PROBLEMS

PROBLEM SOLVING

General Journal

	Date	Account Title	P.R.	Debit	Credit	
1						1
2						2
3						3
4						4
5						5
6						6
7						7
8						8
9						9
10						10
11						11
12						12
13						13
14						14
15						15
16						16

Direct Materials Quantity Variance + Direct Materials Price Variance = Direct Materials Variance

_____ + _____ = _____

Direct Labor Time Variance + Direct Labor Rate Variance = Direct Labor Variance

_____ + _____ = _____

This page intentionally left blank.

COMMUNICATIONS

_____

_____

_____

_____

_____

_____

_____

_____

_____

_____

_____

_____

_____

ETHICS

_____

_____

_____

_____

_____

_____

_____

_____

_____

_____

_____

_____

_____

_____

_____

_____

This page intentionally left blank.

PRACTICE TEST ANSWERS

PART I

1. T
2. T
3. F
4. T
5. F
6. T
7. F
8. F
9. F
10. F
11. T
12. T
13. T
14. T
15. T
16. T
17. T
18. T
19. T
20. T

PART II

1. c
2. j
3. a
4. b
5. i
6. d
7. f
8. h
9. g
10. e

PART III

1. budget
2. standard
3. sales
4. production
5. cash
6. capital expenditures
7. balance sheet
8. flexible
9. variable
10. fixed
11. variance
12. unfavorable
13. quantity
14. time
15. rate

PART IV

1. d
2. a
3. a
4. c
5. c
6. a
7. c
8. b
9. d
10. c

PART V

Answers will vary. Please discuss questions with your instructor.

28 Cost Behavior and Cost-Volume-Profit Analysis

CHAPTER SUMMARY

Cost behavior refers to the way a cost changes (behaves) in relation to changes in an activity level. A variable cost is one that varies in direct proportion to a change in production. When production increases, variable costs increase. On the other hand, when production declines, variable costs will also decline. Direct materials and direct labor are examples of variable costs in a manufacturing firm. The more a firm produces, the more materials and labor are needed.

While variable costs always vary in total with changes in production, they always remain constant on a per unit basis. For example, if a firm is paying its employees $12 an hour, the total labor cost to produce 2,000 units will be twice that to produce 1,000 units. However, the unit cost of $12 stays the same whether the firm produces 1,000 units, 2,000 units, or another quantity.

A fixed cost is one that stays constant in total regardless of the activity level. For example, if a firm is paying $6,000 a month rent on its factory building, the rent will not change just because production goes up or down. A fixed cost is only fixed in total. As production increases, fixed costs per unit go down (because there are more units to spread the fixed costs over). On the other hand, when production falls, fixed costs per unit increase (because there are fewer units to spread the fixed costs over).

A **mixed cost** is one with both variable and fixed characteristics. Utilities such as electricity and natural gas are a good example of a mixed cost. There is a fixed monthly connection charge even if no production at all occurs and no electricity or gas is used. Any amount above the connection charge varies with usage.

For managerial analysis, mixed costs are usually separated into their fixed and variable components. The **high-low method** is one way to do this. Under this method, the highest and lowest activity levels (and the cost at each level) are used to determine the variable and fixed costs. Since total fixed costs do not change during a period, any difference between total costs and total units at the highest (or lowest) level of production during the period is an estimate of the variable costs.

Cost-volume-profit analysis (CVP) is the study of the relationships among costs, selling prices, production volume, expenses, and profits. CVP is a valuable tool in production and product planning.

The **contribution margin** is the excess of sales revenue over variable costs. This is the amount available to cover the fixed costs and provide a profit.

The **contribution margin ratio** is the percentage of each dollar of sales available to cover the fixed costs and to provide operating income. It is computed as follows:

$$\text{Contribution margin ratio} = \frac{\text{Sales} - \text{Variable costs}}{\text{Sales}}$$

The **unit contribution margin** can be used to measure the effect that a change in sales has on operating income; it is computed by subtracting the variable cost per unit from the selling price per unit. If you multiply the unit contribution margin by a certain number, you will obtain the increase (or decrease) in operating income if sales rise (or fall) by that number.

The **break-even point** is the point where sales dollars exactly equal total fixed and variable costs and there is zero profit and zero loss. It is computed as follows:

$$\text{Break-even point in units} = \frac{\text{Fixed costs}}{\text{Unit contribution margin}}$$

When the break-even point in units is multiplied by the unit selling price, the break-even point in dollars results. The break-even point is very important to management because once this point has been reached, any additional sales will provide a profit.

The amount of sales needed for a desired profit can be computed by adding the desired profit to the fixed costs and dividing by the unit contribution margin.

The **margin of safety** is the amount of sales above the break-even point. This measure indicates how far sales can fall before a loss occurs. It is computed as follows:

$$\text{Margin of safety} = \frac{\text{Sales} - \text{Break-even sales}}{\text{Sales}}$$

PRACTICE TEST

PART I TRUE/FALSE

Please circle the correct answer.

T   F   1.   Cost behavior refers to the way a cost changes in relation to a change in the level of production.

T   F   2.   A variable cost is variable on a per unit basis, but is fixed in total.

T   F   3.   A good example of a purely variable cost is straight-line depreciation of factory equipment.

T   F   4.   A fixed cost is fixed on a per unit basis, but is variable in total.

T   F   5.   A good example of a purely fixed cost is direct materials.

T   F   6.   A mixed cost has both variable and fixed characteristics.

T   F   7.   The high-low method uses the highest and lowest activity levels to separate variable and fixed costs.

T   F   8.   When the high-low method is used, the variable cost per unit is calculated as:

$$\frac{\text{Difference in total cost}}{\text{Difference in production}}$$

T   F   9.   Cost-volume-profit analysis is the study of the relationships among costs, selling prices, production volume, expenses, and profits.

T   F   10.   Contribution margin is the excess of variable costs over sales revenue.

T   F   11.   The contribution margin ratio is the percentage of each dollar of sales available to cover the fixed costs and to provide operating income.

T   F   12.   The contribution margin ratio is calculated as:

$$\frac{\text{Sales} - \text{Variable costs}}{\text{Sales}}$$

T   F   13.   The unit contribution margin is the sales price of an item minus the fixed cost per unit.

T   F   14.   If the sales price per unit is $20, the fixed cost per unit is $4, and the variable cost per unit is $8, the unit contribution margin is $8.

T   F   15.   The break-even point is the point where total sales dollars exactly equal total fixed and variable costs and there is no profit or loss.

T   F   16.   The break-even point in units is calculated as:

$$\frac{\text{Variable costs}}{\text{Unit contribution margin}}$$

T   F   17.   The amount of sales needed for a desired profit is calculated as:

$$\frac{\text{Variable costs} + \text{Desired profit}}{\text{Unit contribution margin}}$$

T   F   18.   The margin of safety is the amount of sales above the break-even point.

T   F   19.   The margin of safety is calculated as:

$$\frac{\text{Sales} - \text{Break-even sales}}{\text{Sales}}$$

T   F   20.   The margin of safety indicates how far sales can fall before an operating loss results.

PART II MATCHING

Please match each of the following terms with its definition.

a. break-even point
b. contribution margin
c. contribution margin ratio
d. cost behavior
e. cost-volume-profit analysis

f. fixed cost
g. margin of safety
h. mixed cost
i. unit contribution margin
j. variable cost

_____ 1. Refers to the way a cost changes in relation to a change in the level of production.

_____ 2. A cost that varies in total, but remains constant on a per unit basis.

_____ 3. A cost that is fixed in total, but varies on a per unit basis.

_____ 4. A cost that has both variable and fixed characteristics.

_____ 5. The study of the relationships among costs, selling prices, production volume, expenses, and profits.

_____ 6. The excess of sales revenue over variable costs.

_____ 7. The percentage of each dollar of sales available to cover the fixed costs and to provide operating income.

_____ 8. The sales price of an item minus the variable cost per unit.

_____ 9. The point where total sales dollars exactly equal total fixed and variable costs and there is no profit or loss.

_____ 10. The amount of sales above the break-even point.

PART II FILL IN THE BLANKS

Please complete each sentence with the correct word or words.

1. _____ refers to the way a cost changes in relation to a change in the level of production.

2. A(n) _____ cost will change in _____ based on a change in output, but will always remain _____ on a per unit basis.

3. A(n) _____ cost is fixed in total, but _____ on a per unit basis.

4. A(n) _____ cost has both fixed and variable components.

5. The _____ method uses the highest and lowest activity levels to separate a mixed cost into _____ and _____ costs.

6. _____–_____–_____ analysis is the study of the relationships among costs, selling prices, production volume, expenses, and profits.

7. The _____ is the excess of sales revenue over variable costs.

8. The _____ is the percentage of each dollar of sales available to cover the fixed costs and to provide operating income.

9. The _____ is the point where total sales dollars exactly equal total fixed and variable costs and there is no profit or loss.

10. The _____ is the amount of sales above the break-even point; it indicates how far sales can fall before an operating loss results.

PART IV MULTIPLE CHOICE

Please circle the correct answer.

1. A cost that varies in direct proportion to a change in output or activity level, but will always remain constant on a per unit basis, is a
   a. fixed cost.
   b. variable cost.
   c. mixed cost.
   d. none of the above.

2. A cost that remains the same in total dollar amount as the level of output or activity changes, but varies on a per unit basis, is a
   a. fixed cost.
   b. variable cost.
   c. mixed cost.
   d. none of the above.

3. A cost that has both fixed and variable components is a
   a. fixed cost.
   b. variable cost.
   c. mixed cost.
   d. none of the above.

4. A method of separating a mixed cost into its fixed and variable components, using the highest and lowest activity levels, is known as the
   a. mathematical method.
   b. accounting method.
   c. statistical method.
   d. high-low method.

5. A study of the relationships among costs, selling prices, production volume, expenses, and profits is known as
   a. selling price-production volume analysis.
   b. expense and profit analysis.
   c. cost-volume-profit analysis.
   d. price-volume-expense analysis.

6. The excess of sales revenue over variable costs is called
   a. contribution margin.
   b. gross profit.
   c. net income.
   d. none of the above.

7. The contribution margin ratio is the percentage of each dollar of sales available to cover the fixed costs and to provide operating income. This ratio is calculated as
   a. Sales − Fixed costs ÷ Sales.
   b. Sales − Variable costs ÷ Variable costs.
   c. Sales − Variable costs ÷ Sales.
   d. Variable costs ÷ Sales.

8. The unit sales price of an item minus the variable cost per unit is called the
   a. break-even point.
   b. unit contribution margin.
   c. margin of safety.
   d. mixed cost.

9. The point where total sales dollars exactly equal total fixed and variable costs and there is no profit or loss is called the
   a. margin of safety.
   b. contribution margin.
   c. high-low point.
   d. break-even point.

10. The amount of sales above the break-even point, which indicates how far sales can fall before an operating loss results is called the
   a. margin of safety.
   b. contribution margin.
   c. unit contribution margin.
   d. variable cost.

11. If sales are $100,000, fixed costs are $20,000, and variable costs are $60,000, the contribution margin ratio is
   a. 80%.
   b. 60%.
   c. 40%.
   d. 20%.

12. At 10,000 units produced, the total cost of a product is $50,000; at 5,000 units produced, the total cost is $30,000. Using the high-low method to separate mixed costs, the variable cost per unit is
   a. $10.
   b. $6.
   c. $5.
   d. $4.

13. At 10,000 units produced, the total cost of a product is $50,000; at 5,000 units produced, the total cost is $30,000. Using the high-low method to separate mixed costs, the total cost of 6,500 units produced is
   a. $36,000.
   b. $20,000.
   c. $32,500.
   d. $39,000.

14. For the current year, Johnson Company has variable costs of $80,000, fixed costs of $50,000, a unit selling price of $20, and a unit contribution margin of $5. The firm's break-even point in units is
   a. 16,000.
   b. 10,000.
   c. 4,000.
   d. 2,500.

15. For the current year, Johnson Company has variable costs of $80,000, fixed costs of $50,000, a unit selling price of $20, and a unit contribution margin of $5. The number of units Johnson Company must sell to achieve a desired profit of $25,000 is
   a. 31,000.
   b. 21,000.
   c. 15,000.
   d. 5,000.

PART V WRITING/SHORT ANSWER

1. **Reflect** Make a list, in words or simple phrases, of the most important and meaningful points in this chapter.

2. **Question** Think about the most confusing points or the material you do not understand in this chapter. Write down two or three questions that remain unanswered.

3. **Connect** Explain, in one or two sentences, the connection between the main points of this chapter and the major goals of the entire course.

4. **Summarize** Review this chapter's Joining the Pieces visual summary and explain the concept(s) illustrated in a few sentences.

SKILLS REVIEW

EXERCISE 28-1

(a)

(b)

(c)

EXERCISE 28-2

	Production	**Total Cost**
(a) High	_____	_____
Low	_____	_____
Difference	_____	_____

$$\text{Variable cost per unit} \ = \ \frac{\text{Difference in total cost}}{\text{Difference in production}} \ =$$

(b) Total cost at _____ point (variable and fixed) = _____

Total variable cost at _____ point = _____

Total fixed cost = _____

EXERCISE 28-3

	Sales	_____
	Variable costs	_____
(a)	Contribution margin	_____
	Fixed costs	_____
(b)	Operating income	_____

EXERCISE 28-4

Sales   _____

Variable costs   _____

(a) Contribution margin   _____

(b) Contribution margin ratio = $\dfrac{\text{Sales} - \text{Variable costs}}{\text{Sales}}$ =

(c) Unit selling price   _____

     Unit variable cost   _____

     Unit contribution margin   _____

EXERCISE 28-5

(a) _____

(b) _____

(c) _____

(d) _____

EXERCISE 28-6

(a)

(b)

(c)

(d)

EXERCISE 28-7

(a)

(b)

EXERCISE 28-8

$$\text{Margin of safety} = \frac{\text{Sales} - \text{Break-even sales}}{\text{Sales}} =$$

This page intentionally left blank.

CHALLENGE PROBLEMS

PROBLEM SOLVING

This page intentionally left blank.

COMMUNICATIONS

_____

_____

_____

_____

_____

_____

_____

_____

_____

_____

_____

_____

_____

_____

_____

_____

_____

_____

ETHICS

_____

_____

_____

_____

_____

_____

_____

_____

_____

_____

_____

_____

_____

_____

_____

_____

_____

_____

_____

_____

This page intentionally left blank.

PRACTICE TEST ANSWERS

PART I

1. T
2. F
3. F
4. F
5. F
6. T
7. T
8. T
9. T
10. F
11. T
12. T
13. F
14. F
15. T
16. F
17. F
18. T
19. T
20. T

PART II

1. d
2. j
3. f
4. h
5. e
6. b
7. c
8. i
9. a
10. g

PART III

1. Cost behavior
2. variable, total, constant

3. fixed, varies
4. mixed
5. high-low, variable, fixed
6. Cost-volume-profit
7. contribution margin
8. contribution margin ratio
9. break-even point
10. margin of safety

PART IV

1. b
2. a
3. c
4. d
5. c
6. a
7. c
8. b
9. d
10. a
11. c
12. d
13. a
14. b
15. c

PART V

Answers will vary. Please discuss questions with your instructor.

29 Government and Not-for-Profit Accounting

CHAPTER SUMMARY

Government and not-for-profit accounting is based on a body of generally accepted accounting principles set by the Governmental Accounting Standards Board (GASB). This group provides controls, rules, and standards for accounting procedures and records for state and local governments and other types of not-for-profit organizations, such as colleges and universities, hospitals, libraries, and churches.

A not-for-profit entity must meet specific requirements in order to be sure that its legally adopted budget is adhered to; to check on the current financial condition of the organization; to be certain that laws, rules, and regulations are met; and to evaluate the efficiency and effectiveness of the organization.

Not-for-profit accounting is often referred to as *fund accounting* because all such organizations maintain a number of funds. A **fund** is a fiscal and accounting entity with a self-balancing set of accounts. There are seven types of funds.

The **general fund** provides most of the basic services and accounts for all resources not found in some other fund. A government unit may have one (and only one) general fund. **Special revenue funds** are restricted funds that are used for specific purposes (such as a fund that collects a gasoline tax and uses it for maintenance of streets and highways). **Capital projects funds** are used to account for major projects, such as construction of a building. **Debt service funds** are used to pay the interest and principal on long-term debt that was incurred to finance the purchase of assets or the construction of buildings.

There are two types of proprietary funds: enterprise and internal service. An **enterprise fund** provides a service to others and charges a fee for that service (such as a municipal swimming pool). An **internal service fund** provides a service to other departments or units of the organization (such as an internal print shop).

A **fiduciary fund** accounts for monies held in trust by the government or some other not-for-profit organization. A fiduciary fund that is expendable can spend its principal, whereas a fiduciary fund that is nonexpendable can spend only the earnings on its principal. Fiduciary funds are often restricted to specific purposes.

GASB standards require that government units prepare a Comprehensive Annual Financial Report (CAFR) that discloses the results of operations for the budget period and the current financial position. The financial statements must report the balances in all types of funds and all account groups, together with all revenues and expenditures and the ending fund balances. Statistical tables provide detailed data to support the statements.

Revenue from interfund transfers is an example of an **other financing source**. The expenditure for an interfund transfer is an **other financing use**. Transfer amounts from the general fund are recorded in the **Operating Transfer Out** account. Transfers to the general fund are recorded in the **Operating Transfer In** account. Interfund transfers are called **quasi-external** transactions.

The accounting procedures for the general fund and special revenue funds are illustrated in this chapter. For both types of funds, there are two kinds of journal entries: budgetary and actual. The budgetary accounts are Estimated Revenues, Appropriations, and Encumbrances. When monies are received from other sources, such as interfund transfers, those are also reported; when monies are **expended** to other sources, such as to other funds, those are reported as well. All government funds prepare an **estimated revenues budget**.

The first step in recording the budget is to enter the estimated revenues. Estimated Revenues, a control account, is used for this purpose; its subsidiary ledger accounts list each expected source of revenue separately. Each of these accounts is debited for its share of the estimated revenues. The total is debited to Estimated Revenues and credited to Fund Balance. **Appropriations** are recorded to set aside monies for specific purposes. Appropriations, a control account, is used along with its subsidiary ledger accounts, which list each anticipated expenditure. When money is transferred to other funds (Estimated Other Financing Uses), these transfers are recorded separately. Fund Balance is debited for the total amount credited to Appropriations and Estimated Other Financing Uses.

The difference between the estimated revenues and the appropriations is the fund balance (which hopefully is a credit balance). Assets acquired by government funds (except proprietary funds) are kept in the General Fixed Assets Account Group (GFAAG) rather than being accounted for by each fund separately. Likewise, long-term debt that is incurred is accounted for in the General Long-Term Debt Account Group (GLTDAG) rather than in individual funds (except proprietary funds).

When monies are actually received, Cash is debited and Revenues is credited. The Revenues account is a control account (with a credit balance). The subsidiary ledger accounts for revenues are identical to those in the estimated revenues subsidiary ledger except that the accounts for revenues have credit balances.

As money is spent, it goes through the **encumbrance** procedure. That is, an expected payment (appropriation) becomes actually incurred (a purchase order is issued). A budgetary entry is required to record the encumbrance, and an actual entry is required to record the needed payment. Encumbrances is debited and Reserve for Encumbrances is credited for those monies that have been committed by the purchase order. (Encumbrances is a control account that has subsidiary ledger accounts with debit balances.) When monies are actually to be paid, the encumbrance entry is reversed for the amount of the invoice received. An account called Expenditures is debited, and Vouchers Payable is credited. The Expenditures account, which is used for recording actual payments, is also a control account, and its subsidiary ledger accounts have debit balances.

A comparison of subsidiary ledger account balances will show how much money was anticipated and how much was actually received; how much was set aside (appropriated) and how much was encumbered; and, finally, how much of the encumbered amount was actually spent. Generally, money that is not spent cannot be carried forward; that is, the authority lapses and the money must be returned to the general fund.

All governmental units use a voucher system. When the encumbrance entry occurs, there is a voucher that signals a formal setting aside of committed funds. The actual expenditure may differ from the amount set aside; nevertheless, the Vouchers Payable account is credited at the time the encumbrance is recognized. Vouchers Payable is debited (and Cash is credited) when the actual cash payment is made.

PRACTICE TEST

PART I TRUE/FALSE

Please circle the correct answer.

T   F   1. The accounting procedures and records used by government and not-for-profit organizations are controlled by a group called the Financial Accounting Standards Board (FASB).

T   F   2. GASB standards apply to state and local governments as well as to not-for-profit organizations.

T   F   3. A fund is a fiscal and accounting equity with a self-balancing set of accounts.

T   F   4. There are five major types of funds used in governmental accounting.

T   F   5. The general fund provides most of the basic services and accounts for all resources not found in some other fund.

T   F   6. Generally, all types of funds account for the assets they have acquired and the debt incurred to finance those assets.

T   F   7. A special revenue fund collects monies for a specific purpose, and these monies cannot be used for any other purpose.

T   F   8. A profit is generated by proprietary funds.

T   F   9. Enterprise funds provide services to others and receive revenue for those services (such as the fees collected from the operations of a municipal airport).

T   F   10. An internal service fund provides services to outsiders in a manner similar to an enterprise fund.

T   F   11. Fiduciary funds that are allowed to spend only their earnings are called expendable funds.

T   F   12. The Comprehensive Annual Financial Report (CAFR) is not required for all governmental units.

T   F   13. Estimated Revenues is a budgetary control account with a debit balance.

T   F   14. Appropriations is a budgetary control account with a credit balance.

T   F   15. Governmental and not-for-profit organizations generally use a voucher system to account for all monies expended.

PART II MATCHING

Please match each of the following terms with its definition.

a. fund
b. general fund
c. special revenue fund
d. capital projects fund
e. debt service fund
f. enterprise fund
g. internal service fund
h. proprietary fund

i. expendable fund
j. nonexpendable fund
k. Estimated Revenues
l. Appropriations
m. Encumbrances
n. Expenditures
o. Vouchers Payable
p. quasi-external transactions

_____ 1. A fund used to account for major projects, such as construction of a bridge.

_____ 2. A fiduciary fund that can spend its principal.

_____ 3. A budgetary control account that is used to record all anticipated sources of income for a fund.

_____ 4. A fiscal and accounting entity with a self-balancing set of accounts.

_____ 5. A fund that is used to pay the principal and interest on the long-term debt of a government unit.

_____ 6. A fund that provides most of the basic services and accounts for all resources not found in some other fund.

_____ 7. A budgetary control account with a credit balance that is used to record monies authorized to be spent.

_____ 8. Interfund transfers that result in recognition of revenue and expenditures just as if outside parties were involved.

_____ 9. A fund that accounts for monies that are restricted to a specific purpose, such as highway maintenance.

_____ 10. The budgetary control account that is debited at the time a purchase order or other document making a commitment of funds is issued.

_____ 11. A proprietary fund that provides a service to outside users and charges a fee for that service, such as a municipal transit system.

_____ 12. A fiduciary fund that can spend only the earnings on its principal.

_____ 13. A proprietary fund that provides a service to other departments or units of the organization.

_____ 14. An account that is credited when recording expenditures (actual payments) of money.

_____ 15. A type of fund that uses accrual accounting because it generates a profit and must account for that profit.

_____ 16. A control account that is debited when recording actual monies that are being spent.

PART III FILL IN THE BLANKS

Please complete each sentence with the correct word or words.

1. GASB is a necessary organization because governments serve taxpayers rather than stockholders or owners and have the power to require _____ contributions that may or may not be in proportion to the services received.

2. Government and not-for-profit accounting systems are organized and operated on a(n) _____ basis.

3. The _____ fund provides most of the basic services of government. This fund accounts for all resources not found in some other fund.

4. Government funds do not account for the fixed assets used in their operations; these assets are placed in an account group called the _____ (GFAAG).

5. A(n) _____ fund is a type of proprietary fund that provides a service to outside users and charges a fee for that service.

6. A(n) _____ fund is one that can only spend the earnings on its principal.

7. The budgetary control account called _____ is used to record monies that are authorized to be spent.

8. When a liability is incurred, the appropriation is said to be _____. An encumbrance is then recorded.

9. Estimated Revenues is a(n) _____ control account that is debited for the total anticipated revenues; it is supported by the estimated revenues subsidiary ledger.

10. The _____ budgetary control account and its subsidiary ledger accounts are debited when expected liabilities are recorded.

11. Governmental units use a(n) _____ system to pay amounts owed because it is important that all expenditures be properly authorized before cash is paid.

12. Interfund transfers are said to be _____ because they result in recognition of revenues and expenditures just as if the transactions involved parties outside the governmental unit.

13. When items that were previously encumbered are to be paid, you _____ the Reserve for Encumbrances account and _____ the Encumbrance account.

14. When items are to be paid, you also debit the _____ account and credit _____.

15. When a voucher is paid, the _____ account is debited and Cash is credited.

PART IV MULTIPLE CHOICE

Please circle the correct answer.

1. Which of these is *not* an objective of governmental accounting?
   a. to compare actual results to the budget
   b. to assess current financial condition
   c. to determine whether laws have been complied with
   d. to determine whether or not a profit has been made

2. A fiscal and accounting entity with a self-balancing set of accounts is a(n)
   a. general fund.
   b. fund.
   c. asset account group.
   d. expendable trust.

3. Which of these would be a special revenue fund?
   a. a fund that is responsible for major projects such as construction of a building
   b. a fund that provides in-house printing services
   c. a fund that operates the municipal swimming pool and charges fees to the public
   d. a fund that collects a gasoline tax and uses it for maintenance of highways

4. The fixed assets of governmental units (except for proprietary funds) are accounted for in what way?
   a. Each fund accounts for its own fixed assets.
   b. The fixed assets are not accounted for.
   c. The fixed assets are placed in an account group called General Fixed Assets Account Group.
   d. none of the above

5. Which of these is an internal service fund?
   a. a fund that operates the municipal water and electric utilities and provides service to the public for a fee
   b. a fund that operates a print shop for use by other city departments
   c. a fund that operates the municipal airport and collects fees from users
   d. a fund that operates the public swimming pool and charges fees to users

6. The section of the CAFR that contains the letter of transmittal is
   a. the introductory section.
   b. the financial section.
   c. the statistical tables.
   d. none of the above.

7. GASB standards require that each governmental unit have
   a. no general fund.
   b. one general fund.
   c. two general funds.
   d. as many general funds as are needed.

8. When a liability is incurred, an appropriation is said to be
   a. budgeted.
   b. encumbered.
   c. expended.
   d. spent.

9. Which of these is *not* a budgetary account?
   a. Estimated Revenues
   b. Appropriations
   c. Encumbrances
   d. Expenditures

10. Which of these is *not* a control account?
    a. Estimated Revenues
    b. Appropriations
    c. Expenditures
    d. All of the above are control accounts.

11. Because they result in the recognition of revenues and expenditures as if they were outside transactions, interfund transfers are called
    a. expenses.
    b. expenditures.
    c. quasi-external.
    d. proprietary.

12. When items previously encumbered are actually paid, a debit is made to
    a. Encumbrances.
    b. Reserve for Encumbrances.
    c. Vouchers Payable.
    d. Cash.

PART V WRITING/SHORT ANSWER

1. **Reflect** Make a list, in words or simple phrases, of the most important and meaningful points in this chapter.

2. **Question** Think about the most confusing points or the material you do not understand in this chapter. Write down two or three questions that remain unanswered.

3. **Connect** Explain, in one or two sentences, the connection between the main points of this chapter and the major goals of the entire course.

4. **Summarize** Review this chapter's Joining the Pieces visual summary and explain the concept(s) illustrated in a few sentences.

WORKING PAPERS

SKILLS REVIEW

EXERCISE 29-1

1. _____

_____

_____

_____

_____

_____

2. _____

_____

_____

_____

_____

_____

_____

_____

_____

EXERCISE 29-2

1. _____

2. _____

EXERCISE 29-3

EXERCISE 29-4

	Date		Account Title	P.R.	Debit	Credit	
1							1
2							2
3							3
4							4
5							5
6							6
7							7
8							8
9							9
10							10
11							11
12							12
13							13
14							14
15							15
16							16
17							17
18							18
19							19
20							20
21							21
22							22
23							23
24							24
25							25
26							26
27							27
28							28
29							29
30							30
31							31
32							32

General Journal

	Date	Account Title	P.R.	Debit	Credit	
1						1
2						2
3						3
4						4
5						5
6						6
7						7
8						8
9						9
10						10
11						11
12						12
13						13
14						14
15						15
16						16
17						17
18						18
19						19
20						20
21						21
22						22
23						23
24						24
25						25
26						26
27						27
28						28
29						29
30						30
31						31
32						32

EXERCISE 29-5

	Date	Account Title	P.R.	Debit	Credit	
1						1
2						2
3						3
4						4
5						5
6						6
7						7
8						8
9						9
10						10
11						11
12						12
13						13
14						14
15						15
16						16
17						17
18						18
19						19
20						20
21						21
22						22
23						23
24						24
25						25
26						26
27						27
28						28
29						29
30						30
31						31
32						32

This page intentionally left blank.

CASE PROBLEMS

PROBLEM 29-1A OR 29-1B

I.

General Journal

Page 1

	Date	Account Title	P.R.	Debit	Credit	
1						1
2						2
3						3
4						4
5						5
6						6
7						7
8						8
9						9
10						10
11						11

2.

General Ledger

ACCOUNT **Estimated Revenues**

ACCOUNT NO. **111**

DATE	ITEM	P.R.	DEBIT	CREDIT	BALANCE	
					DEBIT	CREDIT

ACCOUNT **Fund Balance**

ACCOUNT NO. **113**

DATE	ITEM	P.R.	DEBIT	CREDIT	BALANCE	
					DEBIT	CREDIT

Estimated Revenues Ledger

ACCOUNT _____   ACCOUNT NO. 111.1

DATE	ITEM	P.R.	DEBIT	CREDIT	BALANCE	
					DEBIT	CREDIT

ACCOUNT _____   ACCOUNT NO. 111.2

DATE	ITEM	P.R.	DEBIT	CREDIT	BALANCE	
					DEBIT	CREDIT

ACCOUNT _____   ACCOUNT NO. 111.3

DATE	ITEM	P.R.	DEBIT	CREDIT	BALANCE	
					DEBIT	CREDIT

ACCOUNT Miscellaneous Revenue   ACCOUNT NO. 111.4

DATE	ITEM	P.R.	DEBIT	CREDIT	BALANCE	
					DEBIT	CREDIT

PROBLEM 29-2A OR 29-2B

1.

General Journal

Page 1

	Date	Account Title	P.R.	Debit	Credit	
1						1
2						2
3						3
4						4
5						5
6						6
7						7
8						8
9						9
10						10
11						11
12						12
13						13
14						14
15						15
16						16

2.

General Ledger

ACCOUNT Fund Balance   ACCOUNT NO. 113

DATE	ITEM	P.R.	DEBIT	CREDIT	BALANCE	
					DEBIT	CREDIT

ACCOUNT Appropriations   ACCOUNT NO. 211

DATE	ITEM	P.R.	DEBIT	CREDIT	BALANCE	
					DEBIT	CREDIT

ACCOUNT Estimated Other Financing Uses   ACCOUNT NO. 212

DATE	ITEM	P.R.	DEBIT	CREDIT	BALANCE	
					DEBIT	CREDIT

Appropriations Ledger

ACCOUNT General Government   ACCOUNT NO. 211.1

DATE	ITEM	P.R.	DEBIT	CREDIT	BALANCE	
					DEBIT	CREDIT

ACCOUNT Public Safety   ACCOUNT NO. 211.2

DATE	ITEM	P.R.	DEBIT	CREDIT	BALANCE	
					DEBIT	CREDIT

ACCOUNT   ACCOUNT NO. 211.3

DATE	ITEM	P.R.	DEBIT	CREDIT	BALANCE	
					DEBIT	CREDIT

ACCOUNT Parks and Recreation   ACCOUNT NO. 211.4

DATE	ITEM	P.R.	DEBIT	CREDIT	BALANCE	
					DEBIT	CREDIT

ACCOUNT   ACCOUNT NO. 211.5

DATE	ITEM	P.R.	DEBIT	CREDIT	BALANCE	
					DEBIT	CREDIT

Other Financing Uses Ledger

ACCOUNT Operating Transfers Out   ACCOUNT NO. 212.1

DATE	ITEM	P.R.	DEBIT	CREDIT	BALANCE	
					DEBIT	CREDIT

PROBLEM 29-3A OR 29-3B

1.   **General Journal**   Page 1

	Date	Account Title	P.R.	Debit	Credit	
1						1
2						2
3						3
4						4
5						5
6						6
7						7
8						8
9						9
10						10

2.   **General Ledger**

ACCOUNT Cash   ACCOUNT NO. 111

DATE	ITEM	P.R.	DEBIT	CREDIT	BALANCE	
					DEBIT	CREDIT

ACCOUNT Revenues   ACCOUNT NO. 312

DATE	ITEM	P.R.	DEBIT	CREDIT	BALANCE	
					DEBIT	CREDIT

Revenues Ledger

ACCOUNT Licenses and Fees   ACCOUNT NO. 312.1

DATE	ITEM	P.R.	DEBIT	CREDIT	BALANCE	
					DEBIT	CREDIT

ACCOUNT   ACCOUNT NO. 312.2

DATE	ITEM	P.R.	DEBIT	CREDIT	BALANCE	
					DEBIT	CREDIT

ACCOUNT Miscellaneous Revenue   ACCOUNT NO. 312.3

DATE	ITEM	P.R.	DEBIT	CREDIT	BALANCE	
					DEBIT	CREDIT

PROBLEM 29-4A OR 29-4B

1.

General Journal

Page 1

	Date	Account Title	P.R.	Debit	Credit	
1						1
2						2
3						3
4						4
5						5
6						6
7						7
8						8
9						9
10						10
11						11

2.

General Ledger

ACCOUNT Encumbrances   ACCOUNT NO. 113

DATE	ITEM	P.R.	DEBIT	CREDIT	BALANCE	
					DEBIT	CREDIT

ACCOUNT Reserve for Encumbrances   ACCOUNT NO. 114

DATE	ITEM	P.R.	DEBIT	CREDIT	BALANCE	
					DEBIT	CREDIT

PROBLEM 29-4A OR 29-4B (continued)

Encumbrances Ledger

ACCOUNT _____ ACCOUNT NO. _____

DATE	ITEM	P.R.	DEBIT	CREDIT	BALANCE	
					DEBIT	CREDIT

ACCOUNT _____ ACCOUNT NO. _____

DATE	ITEM	P.R.	DEBIT	CREDIT	BALANCE	
					DEBIT	CREDIT

ACCOUNT _____ ACCOUNT NO. _____

DATE	ITEM	P.R.	DEBIT	CREDIT	BALANCE	
					DEBIT	CREDIT

ACCOUNT _____ ACCOUNT NO. _____

DATE	ITEM	P.R.	DEBIT	CREDIT	BALANCE	
					DEBIT	CREDIT

ACCOUNT _____ ACCOUNT NO. _____

DATE	ITEM	P.R.	DEBIT	CREDIT	BALANCE	
					DEBIT	CREDIT

PROBLEM 29-5A OR 29-5B

1.

General Journal

Page 1

	Date	Account Title	P.R.	Debit	Credit	
1						1
2						2
3						3
4						4
5						5
6						6
7						7
8						8
9						9
10						10
11						11
12						12
13						13
14						14
15						15
16						16
17						17

2.

General Ledger

ACCOUNT **Cash**   ACCOUNT NO. **111**

						BALANCE	
DATE	ITEM	P.R.	DEBIT	CREDIT	DEBIT		CREDIT

ACCOUNT **Encumbrances**   ACCOUNT NO. **113**

						BALANCE	
DATE	ITEM	P.R.	DEBIT	CREDIT	DEBIT		CREDIT

ACCOUNT Reserve for Encumbrances   ACCOUNT NO. 114

DATE	ITEM	P.R.	DEBIT	CREDIT	BALANCE DEBIT	BALANCE CREDIT

ACCOUNT Expenditures   ACCOUNT NO. 411

DATE	ITEM	P.R.	DEBIT	CREDIT	BALANCE DEBIT	BALANCE CREDIT

ACCOUNT Vouchers Payable   ACCOUNT NO. 412

DATE	ITEM	P.R.	DEBIT	CREDIT	BALANCE DEBIT	BALANCE CREDIT

Encumbrances Ledger

ACCOUNT General Government   ACCOUNT NO. 113.1

DATE	ITEM	P.R.	DEBIT	CREDIT	BALANCE DEBIT	BALANCE CREDIT

ACCOUNT Public Safety   ACCOUNT NO. 113.2

DATE	ITEM	P.R.	DEBIT	CREDIT	BALANCE DEBIT	BALANCE CREDIT

PROBLEM 29-5A OR 29-5B (continued)

ACCOUNT _____ ACCOUNT NO. _____

DATE	ITEM	P.R.	DEBIT	CREDIT	BALANCE	
					DEBIT	CREDIT

ACCOUNT _____ ACCOUNT NO. _____

DATE	ITEM	P.R.	DEBIT	CREDIT	BALANCE	
					DEBIT	CREDIT

ACCOUNT _____ ACCOUNT NO. _____

DATE	ITEM	P.R.	DEBIT	CREDIT	BALANCE	
					DEBIT	CREDIT

This page intentionally left blank.

PROBLEM SOLVING

General Journal

Page 1

	Date		Account Title	P.R.	Debit	Credit	
1							1
2							2
3							3
4							4
5							5
6							6
7							7
8							8
9							9
10							10
11							11
12							12
13							13
14							14
15							15
16							16
17							17
18							18
19							19
20							20
21							21
22							22
23							23
24							24
25							25
26							26
27							27
28							28
29							29
30							30
31							31
32							32

General Journal

	Date		Account Title	P.R.	Debit	Credit	
1							1
2							2
3							3
4							4
5							5
6							6
7							7
8							8
9							9
10							10
11							11
12							12
13							13
14							14
15							15
16							16
17							17
18							18

COMMUNICATIONS

ETHICS

This page intentionally left blank.

PRACTICE TEST ANSWERS

PART I

1. F
2. T
3. T
4. F
5. T
6. F
7. T
8. T
9. T
10. F
11. F
12. F
13. T
14. T
15. T

PART II

1. d
2. i
3. k
4. a
5. e
6. b
7. l
8. p
9. c
10. m
11. f
12. j
13. g
14. o
15. h
16. n

PART III

1. involuntary
2. fund

3. general
4. General Fixed Assets Account Group
5. enterprise
6. nonexpendable fiduciary
7. Appropriations
8. expended
9. budgetary
10. Encumbrances
11. voucher
12. quasi-external
13. debit, credit
14. Expenditures, Vouchers Payable
15. Vouchers Payable

PART IV

1. d
2. b
3. d
4. c
5. b
6. a
7. b
8. c
9. d
10. d
11. c
12. b

PART V

Answers will vary. Please discuss questions with your instructor.

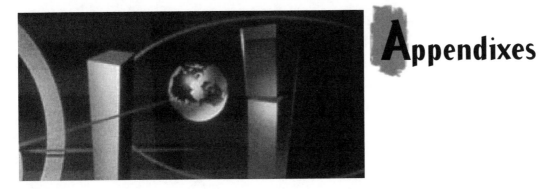

Appendixes

WORKING PAPERS

APPENDIX B

EXERCISE B-1

20X1: _____

20X2: _____

20X3: _____

20X4: _____

EXERCISE B-2

20X1:

20X2:

20X3:

20X4:

20X5:

EXERCISE B-3

First year: _____

Second year: _____

Third year: _____

EXERCISE B-4

First year: _____

Second year: _____

Third year: _____

Fourth year: _____

Fifth year: _____

Sixth year: _____

EXERCISE C-1

General Journal   Page 1

	Date		Account Title	P.R.	Debit	Credit	
1							1
2							2
3							3
4							4
5							5
6							6
7							7
8							8
9							9
10							10
11							11
12							12
13							13
14							14
15							15
16							16
17							17
18							18
19							19
20							20
21							21
22							22
23							23
24							24

1. Job-order costing system   **General Journal**   Page 1

	Date		Account Title	P.R.	Debit	Credit	
1							1
2							2
3							3
4							4
5							5
6							6
7							7
8							8
9							9
10							10
11							11
12							12
13							13
14							14
15							15
16							16
17							17
18							18
19							19
20							20
21							21

EXERCISE C-2 (continued)

2. JIT inventory system

General Journal

Page 1

	Date		Account Title	P.R.	Debit	Credit	
1							1
2							2
3							3
4							4
5							5
6							6
7							7
8							8
9							9
10							10
11							11
12							12
13							13
14							14
15							15
16							16
17							17
18							18
19							19
20							20